Hebrew Bible

Book of
Genesis

Five books of Moses

SimchatChaim.com

The contents of the book

Page   Chapter

Page	Chapter
3.	Introduction to the Jewish Bible
11.	The book of Genesis
17.	**Bereshit**
17.	Chapter 1
19.	Chapter 2
22.	Chapter 3
24.	Chapter 4
26.	Chapter 5
29.	Chapter 6
29.	**Noach**
31.	Chapter 7
33.	Chapter 8
35.	Chapter 9
37.	Chapter 10
40.	Chapter 11
42.	**Lech Lecha**
40.	Chapter 12
44.	Chapter 13
45.	Chapter 14
48.	Chapter 15
49.	Chapter 16
51.	Chapter 17
53.	**Vayera**
53.	Chapter 18
56.	Chapter 19
60.	Chapter 20
62.	Chapter 21
65.	Chapter 22
67.	**Chayei Sara**

Hebrew Bible	Book contents	Book of Genesis
67.	Chapter 23	
67.	Chapter 24	
75.	Chapter 25	
77.		**Toldot**
78.	Chapter 26	
81.	Chapter 27	
86.	Chapter 28	
86.		**Vayetzei**
88.	Chapter 29	
91.	Chapter 30	
95.	Chapter 31	
99.	Chapter 32	
100.		**Vayishlach**
102.	Chapter 33	
104.	Chapter 34	
107.	Chapter 35	
110.	Chapter 36	
113.		**Vayeshev**
113.	Chapter 37	
117.	Chapter 38	
120.	Chapter 39	
122.	Chapter 40	
124.		**Miketz**
124.	Chapter 41	
129.	Chapter 42	
132.	Chapter 43	
136.	Chapter 44	
137.		**Vayigash**
139.	Chapter 45	
141.	Chapter 46	
144.	Chapter 47	
147.		**Vayechi**
148.	Chapter 48	
150.	Chapter 49	
153.	Chapter 50	

Introduction to the

Jewish Bible

First you need to know that the Bible was originally written in the holy language, which today is called Hebrew.

The Tanach itself went through a series of translations from language to language until today's English language.

As a whole, the Tanakh was translated from the holy language into Greek, and from Greek into Latin, and from there into the ancient Agalic, and then into the more modern English.

The problem is when translating from language to language the original meaning is lost.

In the translation of languages there is no realistic possibility to make a completely accurate translation, since in every language there are several translation options for most words, and each word has a different connotation, and also differs to a certain extent from the exact connotation of the original word in the source language.

For example, it is possible to translate the word - שמים. **sky** into English for Sky and Heaven. Two suitable options that each have a different meaning from the other, and also slightly different from the full connotation of the word **sky** שמים. For this reason, along with the attempt to bridge the cultural difference, every translation is actually also an interpretation. In many cases, the translators took the approach of **extensive translation**, in which the translation adds details and interpretations beyond the original text, changes the content, and describes what is happening in a way that is more suitable to the cultural concepts accepted for the period and region. In the common translations these changes are found - to a certain degree of change - in tens of percent of the verses. The general public in these periods knew the Bible only from the translations, and therefore in different regions they actually knew different versions of the same texts, according to the local halachic belief.

The most classic example of this is this:
In the book of Exodus chapter 34 verse 29 it is explained that - KARAN [קרן] the skin of Moses face.

The word KARAN [קרן] has at least two meanings:
A. Radiant.
B. A horn, like that of a bull.
There are other meanings to this word that do not belong to this introduction.

An incorrect translation of the Book of Exodus by Jerome [the Vulgate] into Latin led to an error in the interpretation of the phrase - The horn of the skin of his face. [Exodus 34:29]. And because of this, in

Renaissance sculptures, Moshe's forehead was added **Horns**.

And this is the verse in its entirety according to our translation [compare it to your Bible] - So Moses came down from Mount Sinai. And as Moses came down from the mountain bearing the two tablets of the Pact, Moses was not aware that the skin of his face was **radiant**, since he had spoken with God.

It is known that Hebrew has a vowel for every word. And there can be a word that has a different vowel from the same word. For example, the word with four letters - מ.ד.ב.ר

מְדַבֵּר - speaker.

מִדְבָּר - desert.

מַדְבֵּר - A speaking man.

מִדָּבָר - out of nothing.

מְדֻבָּר - thing that is being discussed.

There are **only** five vowels with the same word, and really this word has 25 vowel types!!!! which can change the entire meaning of the verse and the translation.

The first translations of the Bible were created by Jews at the beginning of the first millennium AD. During this period, most Jews gradually stopped using the Hebrew language, especially biblical Hebrew. A translated Bible became a basic necessity for the reading of the Torah in the synagogues, which was performed by two people - one who read the verse is in the original language, and an interpreter repeats his words in the spoken language.

The first translations of the Bible were created by Jews at the beginning of the first millennium AD. During this period, most Jews gradually stopped using the Hebrew language, especially biblical Hebrew. A translated Bible became a basic necessity for the reading of the Torah in the synagogues, which was performed by two people - one who read the verse is in the original language, and an interpreter repeats his words in the spoken language.

The Bible translations can be divided into two main types - Jewish translations and Christian translations. There are a number of differences between the two, the most prominent of which is the inclusion of the New Testament in Christian translations as opposed to its absence in Jewish translations. The Jewish translations were made mainly from the original Hebrew text, and most of the early Jewish translations were made only into separate parts of the Bible, with the intention that they will be used as a commentary on the Bible. In contrast, the Christian translations are mostly intended for independent use, and most of them are based on the Greek translation translated into Latin - the Latin Vulgate.

The truth is that the Holy Scriptures should not be translated into any language. But because of an act explained in the Talmud there was no choice and the Jews translated it.

And the story is:
And this was due to the incident of King Ptolemy, as it is taught in a Baraita: There was an incident involving King Ptolemy of Egypt, who assembled seventy-two Elders from the Sages of Israel, and put them into seventy-two separate rooms, and did not reveal to them for what purpose he assembled them, so that they would not coordinate their responses. He entered and approached each and every one, and said to each of them: Write for me a translation of the Torah of Moses your teacher. The Holy One, Blessed be He, placed wisdom in the heart of each and every one, and they all agreed to one common understanding. Not only did they all translate the text correctly, they all introduced the same changes into the translated text.

And the Talmud [Megillah 9a] continues to say that all 72 sages did not translate it exactly, but changed several verses, for example:

And they wrote for him: God created in the beginning [**Bereshit**], reversing the order of the words in the first phrase in the Torah that could be misinterpreted as: **Bereshit created God** [Genesis 1:1]. Instead of: Come, let us go down, and there confound their language [Genesis 11:7], which indicates multiple authorities, they wrote in the singular: Come, let me go down, and there confound their language. In addition, they replaced the verse: "And Sarah laughed within herself [**bekirba**] [Genesis 18:12], with: And Sarah laughed among her relatives [**bikroveha**].

They made this change to distinguish between Sarah's laughter, which God criticized, and Abraham's laughter, to which no reaction is recorded. Based on the change, Sarah's laughter was offensive because she voiced it to others....

The church father Hieronymus [about 325-420], who knew Hebrew in addition to Latin and Greek, and specialized in theology, created an improved homogenous translation from all the Latin translations. In his work, which was done between the years 390-405, he was greatly assisted by the Jews he knew. The translation of the first books he dealt with [first prophets, Samuel and kings] was done closely to the Hebrew text, but the last books [Joshua, Judges, Ruth and Esther] were translated by him in a freer manner. In any case, Hieronymus relied on the Hebrew version, because he noticed the deviations that the Greek translations have from the Hebrew original.

The Vulgate was recognized by the Church in 1546 as the authoritative text of the Holy Scriptures. It includes, apart from the books of the Bible and the New Testament, also the translation of the external books. The name **Vulgate** [=Common] can be translated by Roger Bacon, and when the internal division into chapters was made in the Vulgate.

The English translation - a translation of parts of the Bible into English was made starting from the 7th century. A complete translation of the Bible into English, made under the direction of John Wycliffe, from the Latin version of the Vulgate, was published in about 1380. The church condemned this translation, because it saw the interpretation that accompanied it as heretical. Further English translations were also rejected by the church and the king.

In 1530 William Tyndale translated only the Pentateuch from the Greek in the Kaspela edition into English, and 5 years later Miles Coverdale published the entire Bible in English. James I, King of England initiated the creation of an official translation of the Bible and the New Testament into English. His initiative came against the background of the bitter struggle between Protestants and Catholics in England and Scotland. King James proposed to write a new English translation that would be acceptable to Protestants and Catholics alike. This translation, made from Hebrew and Greek, was published in 1611, and is called the "King James Version, KJV". This translation is still considered the authorized translation of the English Bible [Authorized Version]; Researchers from the universities of London, Oxford and Cambridge worked on it. They also used a Jewish commentary for the translation. In this edition, King James demanded to cleanse the kings of any evil that could cling to them, in order to purify the institution of the monarchy. In the translation, an effort was made to maintain the structure of the Hebrew text, and to convert as much as possible a Hebrew word into an English word. However, a Hebrew word may be translated into different words in English in different contexts, this is to keep the language fluid. The attempt to literally translate Hebrew idioms created new expressions in English, which gradually became part of the English language and culture.

The book of Genesis

The book of Genesis is the first book in the books of the Bible. In the Jewish Bible, the book opens the "Torah" section [Five Pentacles of the Torah], and in the Christian Bible, the book is called Γένεσις in the Greek Septuagint translation, or Genesis in the Latin Vulgate translation, and is included in the "Pentateuch" [the five books] in the Old Testament.

According to the Jewish belief in the Torah from Heaven, the writing of the book was done by the hands of Moses, who wrote from the mouth of God.

The contents of the book

Chapters 1 and 2 tell how the world and humans were created: Chapter 1 describes a creation that lasted six days, and was carried out in orderly stages through God's sayings: "Let there be light", "Let there be sky", etc. At the beginning of chapter 2 it is described how with the completion of creation God rested from his work and sanctified the seventh day. In the rest of the chapter, it is told how "on the day the Lord God made the earth and heaven" God created the first man from the earth, then he planted the plants, then he created the animals from the earth and finally the woman from the man's rib. Chapter 3 talks about the sin of the tree of knowledge: Adam and Eve ate the fruit of the forbidden tree of knowledge, and as a result the entire human race was punished. Chapter 4 talks about Cain and Abel, the first sons of Adam and Eve, and how the elder Cain murdered his younger brother Abel because of his jealousy of him. In the rest of the chapter, the histories of the sons of Cain are described.

Chapter 5 begins with the Table of Nations, the family tree from Adam to Noah, and continues with the story of the sin of the sons of God and the deterioration of human morality until God's decision to wipe out the world of humans and animals in a flood, which is recounted in chapters 6-9. God ordered Noah, the only righteous man of that generation, to build an ark and bring his family and all the animals and birds into it, so that they would continue life on earth. Chapter 10 reveals the genealogy of the sons of Noah, in which the genealogies of the peoples who lived in the Middle East and the Near East are detailed.

In chapter 11, it is told how the people sinned in building the Tower of Babel, which is interpreted as daring to face God, and as a result their language became confused and they spread over the entire land. Later in the chapter, the genealogy is detailed from there, the son of Noah to Avraham [Abraham, as it was originally called], the father of nations Many of them the Jewish people.

From here the Jewish nation begins to grow and grow

The stories about Abraham are spread over chapters 12-25, in which it is said that God appeared to Abraham and commanded him to leave his birthplace, Haran, and go to the land of Canaan. He promised Abraham that he would give him the land of Canaan and bless him with many seeds, meaning many descendants. God repeated these promises throughout the multitude of stories centered on Abraham, such as in the covenant between the Bateer's [chapter 15], the covenant of circumcision [chapter 17], and the covenant of Isaac [chapter 22]. Abraham traveled to the land of Canaan, sanctifying it by building altars to God, settled in different places, dug wells and finally bought him and Sarah his wife, a tomb estate in the Cave of the Patriarchs in Hebron [chapter 23]. During his wanderings, Abraham went down to Egypt for a short time due to famine in Canaan, as his great-grandchildren did years later.

The blessing of the seed was fulfilled for the first time when Ishmael, his son from Hagar's family, was born. After that, when he was 100 years old, his son Isaac was born to his wife Sarah, and then he was commanded by God to keep his son Ishmael away, thus marking Isaac as the continuation of the dynasty. At this point the binding of Isaac also happened. Finally, Abraham had the privilege of marrying his son Isaac, and at the end of his days he distinguished him favorably from the other sons of the concubines.

Other stories told as part of the Abraham stories are the story of the war of the four kings and the five, the revolution of Sodom and Gomorrah and the story of the expulsion of Hagar and Ishmael.

Chapters 21-35 talk about Isaac. Although the Bible does not talk much about him, many features in the stories of Abraham are repeated in the stories of Isaac: as his father, he intended to go down from Egypt when famine attacked Canaan, but God commanded him to stay in the land, so he went down to the desert. He quarreled with Abimelech, king of Gerar, due to hiding his relationship with his wife Rebekah, and the Philistines fought with him over water wells, but God was always on his side and he was successful, and finally Abimelech made an alliance with him. At the end of his life, Isaac wanted to bless his eldest son Esau, but Jacob stole the blessings, at the behest of his mother, and got to be blessed in Esau's place.

Isaac is often described as a tolerant person - starting with his dedication, through finding a wife for him, and ending with giving his blessing to Jacob.

The cycle of stories about Jacob and his sons is the longest in the book of Genesis [chapters 25-9]. Jacob, like his father, had to face his brothers for the right of birthright, which means inheriting the land and choosing the father of the nation. He presented himself before his father Isaac, who was angry and accepted His blessing, then fled from Esau to Haran.

In Haran, Jacob had to face his uncle, Laban the Armenian. He married two wives [Leah and Rachel] and two concubines [Bilaha and Zalpha], who bore him 12 sons and a daughter, and returned to the land of Canaan.

During his return to Canaan, Jacob fought alone with the angel of God and defeated him [chapter 32], and because of this he received the name Israel [Yisher-El]. In the land of Canaan, trouble began to come upon him: his daughter Dinah was raped and her brothers killed the rapist and all the people of the city of Nablus, and thus They cast existential fear on the family, and his beloved son Joseph went missing after his brothers sold him into slavery. Afterwards, there was a famine in the land, and his sons went down to Egypt to buy food, where they were accused of spying by the viceroy of Egypt and one of them was even banned, and they were required to bring his little son Benjamin as a ransom.

Finally, it turned out that the missing son, Joseph, is himself the viceroy of Egypt who plotted the plot. All the family members went to live with Joseph in the land of Goshen, and he was kind to them and provided for their livelihood.

The stories of Jacob are combined with the stories of his sons, and the stories of his sons are also combined within each other. The central axis is Joseph, but

Reuben and Yehuda are also protagonists of subplots [the story of Reuben, the story of Yehuda and Tamar, as well as the sale of Joseph]. At the end of the book of Genesis, it is said that Jacob gathered his sons to tell them what would happen to them at the end of time, and blessed each of them with a personal blessing [chapter 39]. In some of the things there are hints of inheriting estates in the Land of Israel in the days of Joshua. Finally, Jacob died in Egypt and was buried in Canaan.

The Book of Genesis was sealed with the death of Joseph and his commanding his brothers to bring his bones to the Promised Land.

Genesis

Bereshit

Chapter 1

1. In the beginning God created the heaven and the earth.

2. The earth was without form and void, and darkness was upon the face of the deep; and the spirit of God hovered over the face of the waters.

3. And God said: Let there be light. And there was light.

4. And God saw the light, that it was good; and God divided the light from the darkness.

5. And God called the light Day, and the darkness He called Night. And there was evening and there was morning, day one.

6. And God said: Let there be an expanse in the midst of the waters, and let it separate the waters from the waters.

7. And God made the expanse, and divided the waters which were under the expanse from the waters which were above the expanse; and it was so.

8. And God called the expanse Heaven. And there was evening and there was morning, day two.

9. And God said: Let the waters under the heaven be gathered together into one place, and let the dry land appear. And it was so.

10. And God called the dry land Earth, and the gathering together of the waters He called Seas; and God saw that it was good.

11. And God said: Let the earth sprout grass, seed

bearing plants, and fruit-trees making fruit according to their kind, from the seeds inside, upon the earth. And it was so.

12. And the earth sprouted grass, seed bearing plants, and trees making fruit according to their kind, from the seeds inside; and God saw that it was good.

13. And there was evening and there was morning, day three.

14. And God said: Let there be lights in the expanse of the heaven to separate the day from the night; and let them be for signs, and for seasons, and for days and years;

15. And let them be for lights in the expanse of the heaven to give light upon the earth. And it was so.

16. And God made the two great lights: the greater light to rule the day, and the lesser light to rule the night; and the stars.

17. And God set them in the expanse of the heaven to give light upon the earth,

18. And to rule over the day and over the night, and to divide the light from the darkness; and God saw that it was good.

19. And there was evening and there was morning, day four.

20. And God said: Let the waters swarm with swarms of living creatures, and let fowl fly above the earth in the open expanse of heaven.

21. And God created the great sea-monsters, and every living creature that creeps, with which the waters swarmed, after its kind, and every winged fowl after its kind; and God saw that it was good.

22. And God blessed them, saying: Be fruitful, and multiply, and fill the waters in the seas, and let fowl multiply in the earth.

23. And there was evening and there was morning, day five.

24. And God said: Let the earth bring forth the living creature after its kind, cattle, and creeping thing, and beast of the earth after its kind. And it was so.

25. And God made the beast of the earth after its kind, and the cattle after their kind, and every thing that creeps upon the ground after its kind; and God saw that it was good.

26. And God said: Let us make man in our image, after our likeness; and let them have dominion over the fish of the sea, and over the fowl of the air, and over the cattle, and over all the earth, and over every creeping thing that creeps upon the earth.

27. And God created man in His own image, in the image of God He created him; male and female He created them.

28. And God blessed them; and God said to them: Be fruitful, and multiply, and replenish the earth, and subdue it; and have dominion over the fish of the sea, and over the fowl of the air, and over every living thing that creeps upon the earth.

29. And God said: Behold, I have given you every plant yielding seed, which is upon the face of all the earth, and every tree, in which is the fruit of a tree yielding seed - to you it shall be for food;

30. And to every beast of the earth, and to every fowl of the air, and to every thing that creeps upon the earth, wherein there is a living soul, I have given every green herb for food. And it was so.

31. And God saw every thing that He had made, and, behold, it was very good. And there was evening and there was morning, day six.

Chapter 2

1. And the heaven and the earth were finished, and all their host.

2. And on the seventh day God finished His work which He had made; and He rested on the seventh day from all His work which He had made.

3. And God blessed the seventh day, and made it holy; because that in it He rested from all His work which God in creating had made.

4. These are the generations of the heaven and of the earth when they were created, in the day that the LORD God made earth and heaven.

5. No shrub of the field was yet in the earth, and no herb of the field had yet sprung up; for the LORD God had not caused it to rain upon the earth, and there was not a man to till the ground;

6. But there went up a mist from the earth, and watered the whole face of the ground.

7. Then the LORD God formed man of the dust of the ground, and breathed into his nostrils the breath of life; and man became a living soul.

8. And the LORD God planted a garden eastward, in Eden; and there He put the man whom He had formed.

9. And out of the ground the LORD God made to grow every tree that is pleasant to the sight, and good for food; the tree of life also in the midst of the garden, and the tree of the knowledge of good and evil.

10. And a river went out of Eden to water the garden; and from there it was parted, and became four heads.

11. The name of the first is Pishon; it encompasses the whole land of Havilah, where there is gold;

12. And the gold of that land is good; there is bdellium and onyx stone.

13. And the name of the second river is Gihon; it encompasses the whole land of Cush.

14. And the name of the third river is Hiddekel [Tigris]; it goes toward the east of Asshur. And the fourth river is the Euphrates.

15. And the LORD God took the man, and put him into the garden of Eden to work it and to keep it.

16. And the LORD God commanded the man, saying: Of every tree of the garden, you may freely eat;

17. But of the tree of the knowledge of good and evil, you shall not eat of it; for in the day that you eat from it you will die.

18. And the LORD God said: It is not good that the man should be alone; I will make him a helper opposite him.

19. And out of the ground the LORD God formed every beast of the field, and every fowl of the air; and brought them to the man to see what he would call them; and whatever the man would call every living creature, that was to be its name.

20. And the man gave names to all cattle, and to the fowl of the air, and to every beast of the field; but for Adam there was not found a helper opposite him.

21. And the LORD God caused a deep sleep to fall upon the man, and he slept; and He took one of his ribs, and closed up the place with its flesh instead.

22. And the rib, which the LORD God had taken from the man, He made a woman, and brought her to the man.

23. And the man said: This is now bone of my bones, and flesh of my flesh; she will be called Woman, because she was taken out of Man.

24. Therefore, a man will leave his father and his mother, and will cleave to his wife, and they will be one flesh.

25. And they were both naked, the man and his wife, and were not ashamed.

Chapter 3

1. Now the snake was naked [**cleverer**] than any beast of the field which the LORD God had made. And he said to the woman: has God said: You shall not eat of any tree of the garden?

2. And the woman said to the serpent: Of the fruit of the trees of the garden we may eat;

3. But of the fruit of the tree which is in the middle of the garden, God has said: You shall not eat of it, neither shall you touch it, or you die.

4. And the serpent said to the woman: You shall not surely die;

5. For God knows that in the day you eat of it, then your eyes shall be opened, and you shall be like God, knowing good and evil.

6. And when the woman saw that the tree was good for food, and that it was a delight to the eyes, and that the tree was to be desired to make one wise, she took of the fruit of it, and ate; and she gave also to her husband with her, and he ate.

7. And both their eyes were opened, and they knew that they were naked; and they sewed fig-leaves together, and made themselves loincloths.

8. And they heard the voice of the LORD God

walking in the garden toward the cool of the day; and the man and his wife hid themselves from the presence of the LORD God among the trees of the garden.

9. And the LORD God called to the man, and said to him: Where are you?

10. And he said: I heard Your voice in the garden, and I was afraid, because I was naked; and I hid myself.

11. And He said: Who told you that you were naked? Have you eaten of the tree, that I commanded you that you should not eat?

12. And the man said: The woman whom You gave to be with me, she gave me of the tree, and I did eat.

13. And the LORD God said to the woman: What is this you have done? And the woman said: The snake tricked me, and I did eat.

14. And the LORD God said to the snake: Because you have done this, you are cursed from among all cattle, and from among all beasts of the field; upon your belly you will go, and you will eat dust all the days of your life.

15. And I will put enmity between you and the woman, and between your seed and her seed; they will bruise your head, and you will bruise their heel.

16. To the woman He said: I will greatly multiply your pain and your distress; in pain you will bring forth children; and your desire will be to your husband, and he shall rule over you.

17. And to Adam He said: Because you have listened to the voice of your wife, and have eaten of the tree, of which I commanded you, saying: You shall not eat of it; cursed is the ground for your sake; in toil you will eat of it all the days of your life.

18. Thorns and thistles it will bring forth to you; and you will eat the herb of the field.

19. By the sweat of your brow you will eat bread, till you return to the ground; for out of it you were taken; for you are dust, and to dust you will return.

20. And the man called his wife's name Eve; because she was the mother of all living.

21. And the LORD God made for Adam and for his wife clothes of skins, and dressed them.

22. And the LORD God said: See, the man is become like one of us, knowing good and evil; and now, he may reach his hand, and take also from the tree of life, and eat, and live for ever.

23. And the LORD God sent him forth from the garden of Eden, to till the ground from which he was taken.

24. So, he drove out the man; and He placed at the east of the garden of Eden the cherubim, and the circling flaming sword, to guard the path to the tree of life.

Chapter 4

1. And the man knew Eve his wife; and she conceived and bore Cain, and said: I have gotten a man with the help of the LORD.

2. And again, she bore his brother Abel. And Abel was a keeper of sheep, but Cain was a tiller of the ground.

3. And in process of time, it came to pass, that Cain brought of the fruit of the ground an offering to the LORD.

4. And Abel, he also brought of the firstlings of his flock and of the fat of it. And the LORD turned to

Abel and to his offering;

5. But to Cain and to his offering He did not turn. And Cain was very angry, and his face fell.

6. And the LORD said to Cain: Why are you angry? and why is your face fallen?

7. If you do well, will it not be lifted up? and if you do not well, sin crouches at the door; and to you is its desire, but you may rule over it.

8. And Cain spoke to Abel his brother. And it came to pass, when they were in the field, that Cain rose up against Abel his brother, and killed him.

9. And the LORD said to Cain: Where is Abel your brother?' And he said: I don't know; am I my brother's keeper?

10. And He said: What have you done? the voice of your brother's blood cries to Me from the ground.

11. And now you are cursed from the ground, which has opened her mouth to receive your brother's blood from your hand.

12. When you till the ground, it shall no more yield to you her strength; a fugitive and a wanderer you will be on the earth.

13. And Cain said to the LORD: My punishment is more than I can bear.

14. See, you have driven me out this day from the face of the land; and from your face shall I be hidden; and I shall be a fugitive and a wanderer in the earth; and it will come to pass, that whoever finds me will kill me.

15. And the LORD said to him: whoever kills Cain, vengeance will be taken on him sevenfold. And the LORD set a sign for Cain, so that none finding him should kill him.

16. And Cain went out from the presence of the LORD, and dwelled in the land of Nod, east of Eden. **17.** And Cain knew his wife; and she conceived, and bore Enoch; and he built a city, and called the name of the city after the name of his son Enoch.

18. And to Enoch was born Irad; and Irad begot Mehujael; and Mehujael begot Methushael; and Methushael begot Lamech.

19. And Lamech took to him two wives; the name of one was Adah, and the name of the other Zillah.

20. And Adah bore Jabal; he was the father of such as dwell in tents and have cattle.

21. And his brother's name was Jubal; he was the father of all such as handle the harp and pipe.

22. And Zillah, she also bore Tubal-cain, the forger of every cutting instrument of brass and iron; and the sister of Tubal-cain was Naamah.

23. And Lamech said to his wives: Adah and Zillah, hear my voice; wives of Lamech, listen to what I say; for I have slain a man for wounding me, And a young man for bruising me;

24. If Cain shall be avenged sevenfold, Lamech will be seventy sevenfold.

25. And Adam knew his wife again; and she bore a son, and named him Seth: for God has appointed me another seed instead of Abel; because Cain killed him.

26. And to Seth, also there was born a son; and he named him Enosh; then men began to call upon the name of the LORD.

Chapter 5

1. This is the book of the generations of Adam. In the

day that God created man, in the likeness of God He made him;

2. Male and female, He created them, and blessed them, and called their name Adam, in the day when they were created.

3. And Adam lived one hundred thirty years, and begot a son in his own likeness, after his image; and called his name Seth.

4. And the days of Adam after he begot Seth were eight hundred years; and he begot sons and daughters.

5. And all the days that Adam lived were nine hundred thirty years; and he died.

6. And Seth lived one hundred five years, and begot Enosh.

7. And Seth lived after he begot Enosh eight hundred seven years, and begot sons and daughters.

8. And all the days of Seth were nine hundred twelve years; and he died.

9. And Enosh lived ninety years, and begot Kenan.

10. And Enosh lived after he begot Kenan eight hundred fifteen years, and begot sons and daughters.

11. And all the days of Enosh were nine hundred five years; and he died.

12. And Kenan lived seventy years, and begot Mahalalel.

13. And Kenan lived after he begot Mahalalel eight hundred forty years, and begot sons and daughters.

14. And all the days of Kenan were nine hundred ten years; and he died.

15. And Mahalalel lived sixty-five years, and begot Jared.

16. And Mahalalel lived after he begot Jared eight hundred thirty years, and begot sons and daughters.

17. And all the days of Mahalalel were eight hundred ninety-five years; and he died.

18. And Jared lived one hundred sixty-two years, and begot Enoch.

19. And Jared lived after he begot Enoch eight hundred years, and begot sons and daughters.

20. And all the days of Jared were nine hundred sixty and two years; and he died.

21. And Enoch lived sixty and five years, and begot Methuselah.

22. And Enoch walked with God after he begot Methuselah three hundred years, and begot sons and daughters.

23. And all the days of Enoch were three hundred sixty-five years.

24. And Enoch walked with God, and he was no more; because God took him.

25. And Methuselah lived a hundred eighty-seven years, and begot Lamech.

26. And Methuselah lived after he begot Lamech seven hundred eighty-two years, and begot sons and daughters.

27. And all the days of Methuselah were nine hundred sixty-nine years; and he died.

28. And Lamech lived one hundred eighty-two years, and begot a son.

29. And he named him Noach, saying - This same shall comfort us in our work and in the toil of our hands, which comes from the ground which the LORD has cursed.

30. And Lamech lived after he begot Noach five hundred ninety and five years, and begot sons and daughters.

31. And all the days of Lamech were seven hundred seventy-seven years; and he died.

32. And Noach was five hundred years old; and Noach begot Shem, Ham, and Japheth.

Chapter 6

1. And it came to pass, when men began to multiply on the face of the earth, and daughters were born to them.

2. That the sons of God saw the daughters of men that they were fair; and they took them wives, whoever they chose.

3. And the LORD said - My spirit shall not abide in man forever, for he also is flesh; so his days shall be a hundred and twenty years.

4. The Nephilim were in the earth in those days, and also after that, when the sons of God came into the daughters of men, and they bore children to them; the same were the mighty men that were of old, the men of renown.

5. And the LORD saw that the wickedness of man was great in the earth, and that every imagination of the thoughts of his heart was only evil continually.

6. And it grieved the LORD that He had made man on the earth, and it grieved Him in His heart.

7. And the LORD said: I will blot out man who I have created from the face of the earth; man, and beast, and creeping thing, and fowl of the air; for it grieves Me that I have made them.

8. But Noach found favor in the eyes of the LORD.

Noach

9. These are the generations of Noach. Noach was in

his generations a man righteous and wholehearted; Noach walked with God.

10. And Noach begot three sons, Shem, Ham, and Japheth.

11. And the earth was corrupt before God, and the earth was filled with violence.

12. And God saw the earth, and it was corrupt; for all flesh had corrupted their way upon the earth.

13. And God said to Noach - The end of all flesh is come before Me; for the earth is filled with violence through them; and I will destroy them with the earth.

14. Make an ark of gopher wood; with rooms you will make the ark, and pitch it inside and outside with pitch.

15. And this is how you will make it: the length of the ark: three hundred cubits, the breadth of it: fifty cubits, and the height of it: thirty cubits.

16. A you will make a skylight in the ark, and you will finish it to a cubit upward; and you will set the door of the ark in the side of it; you will make it with lower, second, and third stories.

17. And I, I do bring the flood of waters upon the earth, to destroy all flesh, in which there is the breath of life, from under heaven; everything that is in the earth shall perish.

18. But I will establish My covenant with you; and you will come into the ark, you, and your sons, and your wife, and your sons' wives with you.

19. And of every living thing of all flesh, you will bring two of every sort into the ark, to keep them alive with you; they will be male and female.

20. Of the fowl after their kind, and of the cattle after their kind, of every creeping thing of the ground after its kind, two of every sort will come to you, to keep them alive.

21. And take with you of all food that is eaten, and gather it to you; and it will be for food for you, and for them.

22. And Noach did everything that God commanded him, it was so.

Chapter 7

1. And the LORD said to Noach - You and all your house Come into the ark; because I have seen you as righteous before Me in this generation.

2. Of every clean beast you shall take to you seven and seven, each with his mate; and of the beasts that are not clean two [and two], each with his mate;

3. Also, of the fowl of the air, seven and seven, male and female; to keep their seed alive on the face of all the earth.

4. Because in seven days, I will cause it to rain upon the earth forty days and forty nights; and every living thing that I have made, I will blot out from the face of the earth.

5. And Noach did everything that the LORD commanded him.

6. And Noach was six hundred years old when the flood of waters was on the earth.

7. And Noach, and his sons, and his wife, and his sons wives, went with him into the ark, because of the waters of the flood.

8. Of clean beasts, and of beasts that are not clean, and of fowls, and of every thing that creeps on the ground,

9. There went two and two to Noach into the ark, male

and female, as God commanded Noach.

10. And in seven days, that the waters of the flood were on the earth.

11. In the six hundredth year of Noach's life, in the second month, on the seventeenth day of the month, on the same day were all the springs of the great deep split, and the windows of heaven were opened.

12. And the rain was upon the earth forty days and forty nights.

13. The same day Noach, and Shem, and Ham, and Japheth, the sons of Noach, and Noach's wife, and the three wives of his sons entered with them, into the ark;

14. They, and every beast of its kind, and all the cattle after their kind, and every creeping thing that creeps upon the earth of its kind, and every fowl of its kind, every bird of every sort.

15. And they went to Noach, into the ark, two and two of all flesh containing the breath of life.

16. And they went in male and female of all flesh, as God commanded him; and the LORD shut him in.

17. And the flood was forty days on the earth; and the waters increased, and lifted up the ark, and it was raised above the earth.

18. And the waters prevailed, and increased greatly on the earth; and the ark went upon the face of the waters.

19. And the waters prevailed exceedingly upon the earth; and all the high mountains that were under the whole heaven were covered.

20. Fifteen cubits upward the waters prevailed; and the mountains were covered.

21. And all flesh that moved upon the earth perished,

fowl, and cattle, and beast, and every swarming thing that swarmed upon the earth, and every man;

22. All who had the breath of the spirit of life in their nostrils, everything that was on the dry land, died.

23. And He blotted out every living thing which was upon the face of the ground, man, and cattle, and creeping things, and fowl of the heaven; and they were blotted out from the earth; and only Noach was left, and those that were with him in the ark.

24. And the waters prevailed on the earth a hundred fifty days.

Chapter 8

1. And God remembered Noach, and every living thing, and all the cattle that were with him in the ark; and God made a wind to pass over the earth, and the waters receded.

2. Also, the springs of the deep and the windows of heaven were stopped, and the rain from heaven was restrained.

3. And the waters receded from off the earth; and after the end of a hundred and fifty days the waters decreased.

4. And the ark rested in the seventh month, on the seventeenth day of the month, on the mountains of Ararat.

5. And the waters receded continually until the tenth month; in the tenth month, on the first day of the month, the tops of the mountains were visible.

6. After forty days, Noach opened the window of the ark he had made.

7. And he sent out a raven, and it went out here and there, until the waters were dried up off the earth.

8. And he sent out a dove, to see if the waters had receded from off the face of the ground.

9. But the dove found no place to rest the sole of its foot, and it returned to him in the ark, for the waters were on the face of the whole earth; and he put out his hand, and took it, and brought it to him into the ark.

10. And he waited still another seven days; and again, he sent out the dove from the ark.

11. And the dove came to him the evening; and in its mouth it had a freshly plucked olive-leaf; so, Noach knew that the waters had receded from the earth.

12. And he waited still another seven days; and sent out the dove; and it did not return to him any more.

13. And it came to pass in the six hundred and first year, in the first month, the first day of the month, the waters were dried up from off the earth; and Noach removed the covering of the ark, and looked and the face of the ground was dry.

14. And in the second month, on the twenty-seventh day of the month, the earth was dry.

15. And God spoke to Noach, saying:

16. Go out of the ark, you, and your wife, and your sons, and your sons' wives with you.

17. Bring out with you every living thing that is with you of all flesh, fowl, and cattle, and every creeping thing that creeps upon the earth; that they may swarm in the earth, and be fruitful, and multiply upon the earth.

18. And Noach went out, and his sons, and his wife, and his sons' wives with him;

19. Every beast, every creeping thing, and every fowl, whatever moves upon the earth, after their families; went out of the ark.

20 And Noach built an altar to the LORD; and took of every clean beast, and of every clean fowl, and offered burnt-offerings on the altar.

21. And the LORD smelled the sweet odor; and the LORD said in His heart: I will never again curse the ground for man's sake; for the imagination of man's heart is evil from his youth; and I will never again kill every thing living, as I have done.

22. While the earth remains, seedtime and harvest, and cold and heat, and summer and winter, and day and night shall not cease.

Chapter 9

1. And God blessed Noach and his sons, and said to them - Be fruitful and multiply, and replenish the earth.

2. And the fear of you and the dread of you shall be upon every beast of the earth, and upon every fowl of the air, and upon everything the creeps on the ground, and upon all the fishes of the sea: into your hand are they delivered.

3. Every moving thing that lives shall be food for you; as the green herbs I have given you all.

4. But flesh with its soul, its blood, you shall not eat.

5. But your blood of your soul I shall require; at the hand of every beast will I require it; and at the hand of man, even at the hand of every man's brother, I will require the soul of man.

6. Whoever Sheds man's blood, by man will his blood be shed; for in the image of God He made man.

7. And you, be fruitful, and multiply; swarm on the earth, and multiply in it.

8. And God spoke to Noach, and to his sons with him,

saying:

9. As for Me, I establish My covenant with you, and with your seed after you;

10. And with every living creature that is with you, the fowl, the cattle, and every beast of the earth with you; of all that go out of the ark, even every beast of the earth.

11. And I will establish My covenant with you; no more will all flesh be cut off by the waters of the flood; and no more will there be a flood to destroy the earth.

12. And God said: This is the sign of the covenant which I make between Me and you and every living creature that is with you, for all the generations of the world:

13. I have set My bow in the cloud, and it shall be for a sign of a covenant between Me and the earth.

14. In the future, when I bring clouds over the earth, and the bow is seen in the cloud,

15. I will remember My covenant, which is between Me and you and every living creature of all flesh; and the waters will no more flood to destroy all flesh.

16. And the bow will be in the cloud; and I will look upon it, that I may remember the everlasting covenant between God and every living creature of all flesh that is on the earth.

17. And God said to Noach: This is the sign of the covenant which I have established between Me and all flesh that is on the earth.

18. And the sons of Noach, that went out of the ark, were Shem, and Ham, and Japheth; and Ham is the father of Canaan.

19. These three were the sons of Noach, and from

these, the whole earth spread out.

20. And Noach, a man of the soil planted a vineyard.

21. And he drank of the wine, and was drunk; and he was uncovered within his tent.

22. And Ham, the father of Canaan, saw the nakedness of his father, and told his two brothers outside.

23. And Shem and Japheth took a garment, and laid it upon both their shoulders, and went backward, and covered the nakedness of their father; and their faces were backward, and they did not see their father's nakedness.

24. And Noach awoke from his wine, and knew what his youngest son had done to him.

25. And he said: Cursed be Canaan; a servant of servants he will be to his brothers.

26. And he said: Blessed be the LORD, the God of Shem;

27. And let Canaan be their servant. God enlarge Japheth, and he will dwell in the tents of Shem; And let Canaan be their servant.

28. And Noach lived after the flood three hundred and fifty years.

29. And all the days of Noach were nine hundred fifty years; and he died.

Chapter 10

1. Now these are the generations of the sons of Noach: Shem, Ham, and Japheth; and sons were born to them after the flood.

2. The sons of Japheth: Gomer, and Magog, and Madai, and Javan, and Tubal, and Meshech, and Tiras.

3. And the sons of Gomer: Ashkenaz, and Riphath, and Togarmah.

4. And the sons of Javan: Elishah, and Tarshish, Kittim, and Dodanim.

5. Of these were the isles of the nations divided in their lands, after his tongues, after their families, in their nations.

6. And the sons of Ham: Cush, and Mizraim, and Put, and Canaan.

7. And the sons of Cush: Seba, and Havilah, and Sabtah, and Raamah, and Sabteca; and the sons of Raamah: Sheba, and Dedan.

8. And Cush begot Nimrod; he began to be a mighty one in the earth.

9. He was a mighty hunter before the LORD; of whom it is said: Like Nimrod a mighty hunter before the LORD.

10. And the beginning of his kingdom was Babel, and Erech, and Accad, and Calneh, in the land of Shinar.

11. Out of that land came Asshur, and built Nineveh, and Rehoboth-ir, and Calah,

12. And Resen between Nineveh and Calah-which is also called the great city.

13. And Mizraim begot Ludim, and Anamim, and Lehabim, and Naphtuhim,

14. And Pathrusim, and Casluhim - from where the Philistines came - and Caphtorim.

15. And Canaan begot Zidon his firstborn, and Heth;

16. And the Jebusite, and the Amorite, and the Girgashite;

17. And the Hivite, and the Arkite, and the Sinite;

18. And the Arvadite, and the Zemarite, and the Hamathite; and afterward were the families of the

Canaanite spread abroad.

19. And the border of the Canaanite was from Zidon, as you go toward Gerar, to Gaza; as you go toward Sodom and Gomorrah and Admah and Zeboiim, to Lasha.

20. These are the sons of Ham, after their families, after their tongues, in their lands, in their nations.

21. And to Shem, the father of all the children of Eber, the elder brother of Japheth, children were also born to him.

22. The sons of Shem: Elam, and Asshur, and Arpachshad, and Lud, and Aram.

23. And the sons of Aram: Uz, and Hul, and Gether, and Mash.

24. And Arpachshad begot Shelah; and Shelah begot Eber.

25. And to Eber were born two sons; the name of the one was Peleg; for in his days was the earth divided; and his brother's name was Joktan.

26. And Joktan begot Almodad, and Sheleph, and Hazarmaveth, and Jerah;

27. And Hadoram, and Uzal, and Diklah;

28. And Obal, and Abimael, and Sheba;

29. And Ophir, and Havilah, and Jobab; all these were the sons of Joktan.

30. And their dwelling was from Mesha, as you go toward Sephar, to the mountain of the east.

31. These are the sons of Shem, after their families, after their tongues, in their lands, after their nations.

32. These are the families of the sons of Noach, after their generations, in their nations; and of these were the nations divided in the earth after the flood.

Chapter 11

1. It happened that the whole earth was of one language and the same words.

2. And it came to pass, as they journeyed east, that they found a valley in the land of Shinar; and they dwelled there.

3. And they said one to another: Come, let us make brick, and burn them thoroughly. And they had brick for stone, and clay for mortar.

4. And they said: Come, let us build us a city, and a tower, with its top in the heavens, and let us make a name for ourselves; so, we won't be scattered across the face of the earth.

5. And the LORD came down to see the city and the tower, which the children of men built.

6. And the LORD said: They are one people, and they have one language; and this is what they begin to do; and now nothing will be withheld from them, which they plan to do.

7. Come, let us go down, and there confuse their language, that they may not understand one another's speech.

8. So, the LORD scattered them abroad from there across the face of the whole earth; and they stopped building the city.

9. So, the name of it was called Babel; because the LORD confused the language of all the earth; and from there the LORD scattered them across the face of the whole earth.

10. These are the generations of Shem. Shem was a hundred years old, and begot Arpachshad two years after the flood.

11. And Shem lived after he begot Arpachshad five

hundred years, and begot sons and daughters.

12. And Arpachshad lived thirty-five years, and begot Shelah.

13. And Arpachshad lived after he begot Shelah four hundred three years, and begot sons and daughters.

14. And Shelah lived thirty years, and begot Eber.

15. And Shelah lived after he begot Eber four hundred three years, and begot sons and daughters.

16. And Eber lived thirty-four years, and begot Peleg.

17. And Eber lived after he begot Peleg four hundred thirty years, and begot sons and daughters.

18. And Peleg lived thirty years, and begot Reu.

19. And Peleg lived after he begot Reu two hundred nine years, and begot sons and daughters.

20. And Reu lived thirty-two years, and begot Serug.

21. And Reu lived after he begot Serug two hundred seven years, and begot sons and daughters.

22. And Serug lived thirty years, and begot Nahor.

23. And Serug lived after he begot Nahor two hundred years, and begot sons and daughters.

24. And Nahor lived twenty-nine years, and begot Terah.

25. And Nahor lived after he begot Terah one hundred nineteen years, and begot sons and daughters.

26. And Terah lived seventy years, and begot Abram, Nahor, and Haran.

27. Now these are the generations of Terah. Terah begot Abram, Nahor, and Haran; and Haran begot Lot.

28. And Haran died in the presence of his father Terah in the land of his birth, in Ur of the Chaldees.

29. And Abram and Nahor took wives: the name of Abram's wife was Sarai; and the name of Nahor's wife, Milcah, the daughter of Haran, the father of Milcah, and the father of Iscah.

30. And Sarai was barren; she had no child.

31. And Terah took Abram his son, and Lot the son of Haran, his son's son, and Sarai his daughter-in-law, his son Abram's wife; and they took them from Ur of the Chaldees, to go to the land of Canaan; and they came to Haran, and dwelled there.

32. And the days of Terah were two hundred five years; and Terah died in Haran.

Lech Lecha

Chapter 12

1. Now the LORD said to Abram: Go out out of your country, and away from your family, and away from your father's house, to the land that I will show you.

2. And I will make you a great nation, and I will bless you, and make your name great; and you will be a blessing.

3. And I will bless those who bless you, and I will curse those that curse you; and in you all the families of the earth will be blessed.

4. So, Abram went, as the LORD had spoken to him; and Lot went with him; and Abram was seventy-five years old when he went out of Haran.

5. And Abram took Sarai his wife, and Lot his brother's son, and all their belongings that they had gathered, and the souls that they had acquired in Haran; and they went out to go to the land of Canaan; and into the land of Canaan they came.

6. And Abram passed through the land to the place of Shechem, to the tree of Moreh. And the Canaanites were in the land then.

7. And the LORD appeared unto Abram, and said: To your seed I will give this land; and there he built an altar to the LORD, who appeared to him.

8. And he moved from there to the mountain on the east of Beth-el, and pitched his tent, having Beth-el to the west, and Ai to the east; and there he built an altar to the LORD, and called upon the name of the LORD.

9. And Abram journeyed on, towards the South.

10. And there was a famine in the land; and Abram went down into Egypt to sojourn there; for the famine was harsh in the land.

11. And it came to pass, when he came near to entering Egypt, he said to Sarai his wife: Now, I know that you are a woman of beautiful appearance.

12. And it will be, when the Egyptians shall see you, that they will say: This is his wife; and they will kill me, but you they will keep alive.

13. Please say, you are my sister; that it may be better for me, for your sake, and that my soul may live because of you.

14. Now, when Abram came to Egypt, the Egyptians saw the woman, that she was very beautiful.

15. And the princes of Pharaoh saw her, and praised her to Pharaoh; and the woman was taken into Pharaoh's house.

16. And he dealt well with Abram for her sake; and he had sheep, and oxen, and he-donkeys, and men-servants, and maid-servants, and she-donkeys, and camels.

17. And the LORD plagued Pharaoh and his house with great plagues because of Sarai Abram's wife.

18. And Pharaoh called Abram, and said: What is this

that you have done to me? Why did you not tell me that she was your wife?

19. Why did you say: She is my sister? so that I took her to be my wife; now here is your wife, take her, and go your way.

20. And Pharaoh commanded men concerning him; and they escorted him on the way, and his wife, and all that he had.

Chapter 13

1. And Abram went up out of Egypt, he, and his wife, and all that he had, and Lot with him, to the South.

2. And Abram was very rich in cattle, in silver, and in gold.

3. And he went on his journeys from the South even to Beth-el, to the place where his tent had been at the beginning, between Beth-el and Ai;

4. To the place of the altar, which he had made there at the first; and Abram called there on the name of the LORD.

5. And Lot, who also went with Abram, had flocks, and herds, and tents.

6. And the land was not able to support them, that they might dwell together; for their possessions was great, so that they could not dwell together.

7. And there was a strife between the herdsmen of Abram's cattle and the herdsmen of Lot's cattle. And the Canaanite and the Perizzite lived in the land then.

8. And Abram said to Lot: Let there be no strife, between me and you, and between my herdsmen and your herdsmen; for we are brothers.

9. Is not the whole land before you? separate yourself, from me; if you go left, then I will go to the right; or if you go right, then I will go to the left.

10. And Lot lifted up his eyes, and saw all the plains of the Jordan, that it was well watered every where, before the LORD destroyed Sodom and Gomorrah, like the garden of the LORD, like the land of Egypt, as you go toward Zoar.

11. So, Lot chose all the plain of the Jordan; and Lot journeyed east; and they separated from one another.

12. Abram dwelled in the land of Canaan, and Lot dwelled in the cities of the Plain, and moved his tent as far as Sodom.

13. Now the men of Sodom were wicked and very sinful against the LORD.

14. And the LORD said to Abram, after Lot was separated from him: Lift up your eyes, and look from the place where you are, northward and southward and eastward and westward;

15. For all the land which you see, I will give it to you, and to your seed for ever.

16. And I will make your seed like the dust of the earth; so that if a man can count the dust of the earth, your seed will also be counted.

17. Arise, walk through the land in the length of it and in the breadth of it; for I will give it to you.

18. And Abram moved his tent, and came and dwelled by the trees of Mamre, which are in Hebron, and built an altar there to the LORD.

Chapter 14

1. In the days of Amraphel king of Shinar, Arioch king of Ellasar, Chedorlaomer king of Elam, and Tidal king of Goiim,

2. That they made war with Bera king of Sodom, and

with Birsha king of Gomorrah, Shinab king of Admah, and Shemeber king of Zeboiim, and the king of Bela - also called Zoar.

3. They came as allies to the valley of Siddim, also called the Salt Sea.

4. Twelve years they served Chedorlaomer, and in the thirteenth year they rebelled.

5. And in the fourteenth year Chedorlaomer came and the kings that were with him, and killed the Rephaim in Ashteroth-karnaim, and the Zuzim in Ham, and the Emim in Shaveh-kiriathaim,

6. And the Horites in mount Seir, to El-paran, which is by the desert.

7. And they turned back, and came to En-mishpat - which is Kadesh - and killed all the country of the Amalekites, and also the Amorites, that dwelt in Hazazon-tamar.

8. And there the king of Sodom went out, and the king of Gomorrah, and the king of Admah, and the king of Zeboiim, and the king of Bela - which is Zoar; and they met in battle against them in the valley of Siddim;

9. Against Chedorlaomer, king of Elam, and Tidal king of Goiim, and Amraphel king of Shinar, and Arioch king of Ellasar; four kings against the five.

10. Now the valley of Siddim was full of clay pits; and the kings of Sodom and Gomorrah fled, and they fell there, and the remaining men fled to the mountain.

11. And they took all the possessions of Sodom and Gomorrah, and all their food, and went their way.

12. And they took Lot, Abram's brother's son, who lived in Sodom, and his possessions, and departed.

13. And one prisoner that had escaped came, and told Abram the Hebrew - now he dwelt by the tree of Mamre the Amorite, brother of Eshcol, and brother of Aner; and these were in alliance with Abram.

14. And when Abram heard that his brother was taken captive, he led his trained men, born in his house, three hundred eighteen, and pursued as far as Dan.

15. And he divided himself against them by night, he and his servants, and killed them, and pursued them to Hobah, which is on the left hand of Damascus.

16. And he brought back all the possessions, and also brought back his brother Lot, and his possessions, and the women, and the people.

17. And the king of Sodom went out to meet him, after his return from the slaughter of Chedorlaomer and the kings that were with him, at the valley of Shaveh - also called the King's Valley.

18. And Melchizedek king of Salem brought bread and wine; and he was priest of God the Most High.

19. And he blessed him, and said: Blessed is Abram of God Most High, Maker of heaven and earth;

20. And blessed is God the Most High, who has delivered your enemies into your hand. And he gave him a tenth of all.

21. And the king of Sodom said to Abram: Give me the people, and take the goods to yourself.

22. And Abram said to the king of Sodom: I have lifted up my hand to the LORD, God Most High, Maker of heaven and earth,

23. I will not take a thread or a shoe-lace or anything that is yours, so you won't say: I have made Abram rich;

24. Except what the young men have eaten, and the

share of the men who went with me, Aner, Eshcol, and Mamre, let them take their portion.

Chapter 15

1. After these things the word of the LORD came to Abram in a vision, saying: Do not fear, Abram, I am your shield, your reward will be exceeding great.

2. And Abram said: O Lord GOD, what will you give me, I go childless, and the inheritor of my house is its steward, Eliezer of Damascus?

3. And Abram said: You have given no seed to me, and no one born in my house is its inheritor.

4. And, the word of the LORD came to him, saying: This man will not be your heir; but one that will come from inside you, will be your inheritor.

5. He brought him out, and said: Look toward heaven, and count the stars, if you are able to count them; and He said to him: So, will your seed be.

6. And he believed in the LORD; and He considered it righteousness for him.

7. And He said to him: I am the LORD that brought you out of Ur of the Chaldees, to give you this land to inherit it.

8. And he said: O Lord GOD, how will I know that I shall inherit it?

9. And He said to him: For Me, take three heifers, and three she-goats, and three rams, and a turtle-dove, and a young pigeon.

10. And he took these, and cut them down the middle, and laid each half against the other; but he did not cut the birds.

11. And the birds of prey came down upon the carcasses, and Abram drove them away.

12. It happened that, when the sun was going down, Abram fell into a deep sleep; and, a fear, a great darkness, descended on him.

13. And He said to Abram: Know for certain that your seed will be a stranger in a land that is not theirs, and they will made servants; and they will afflict them for four hundred years;

14. And I will also judge that nation, whom they will serve; and afterward they will come out with great possessions.

15. But you will go to your fathers in peace; you will be buried in a good old age.

16. And the fourth generation will return here; for the iniquity of the Amorite is not complete yet.

17. And it happened, that, when the sun went down, and there was thick darkness, - a smoking furnace, and a flaming torch that passed between these pieces.

18. In that day the LORD made a covenant with Abram, saying: To your seed I have given this land, from the river of Egypt to the great river, the river Euphrates;

19. the Kenite, and the Kenizzite, and the Kadmonite,

20. And the Hittite, and the Perizzite, and the Rephaim,

21. And the Amorite, and the Canaanite, and the Girgashite, and the Jebusite.

Chapter 16

1. Now Sarai, Abram's wife bore him no children; and she had a handmaid, an Egyptian, whose name was Hagar.

2. And Sarai said to Abram: now, the LORD has restrained me from bearing; please come to my handmaid; it may be that I will be built up through her. And Abram listened to the voice of Sarai.

3. And Sarai Abram's wife took Hagar the Egyptian, her handmaid, after Abram had lived ten years in the land of Canaan, and gave her to Abram, her husband to be his wife.

4. And he went to Hagar, and she conceived; and when she saw that she had conceived, her mistress was lowered in her eyes.

5. And Sarai said to Abram: My wrong be upon you: I gave my handmaid into your lap; and when she saw that she had conceived, I was lowered in her eyes: the LORD judge between me and you.

6. But Abram said to Sarai: Your maid is in your hand; do to her that what is good in your eyes. And Sarai dealt harshly with her, and she fled from her face.

7. And the angel of the LORD found her by a fountain of water in the wilderness, by the fountain on the way to Shur.

8. And he said: Hagar, Sarai's handmaid, where do you come from? and where do you go? And she said: I flee from the face of my mistress Sarai.

9. And the angel of the LORD said unto her: Return to your mistress, and submit yourself under her hands.

10. And the angel of the LORD said to her: I will greatly multiply your seed, that it can not be counted for its multitude.

11. And the angel of the LORD said to her: you are with child, and will bear a son; and you will name him Ishmael, because the LORD has heard your affliction.

12. And he will be a wild donkey of a man: his hand will be against every man, and every man's hand against him; and he will live in the face of all his brothers.

13. And she called the name of the LORD that spoke to her, you are a God of seeing; for she said: Have I even here seen Him that sees Me?

14. So, the well was called **Beer-lahai-roi**; it is between Kadesh and Bered.

15. And Hagar bore Abram a son; and Abram named his son, whom Hagar bore, Ishmael.

16. And Abram was eighty-six years old, when Hagar bore Ishmael to Abram.

Chapter 17

1. And when Abram was ninety-nine years old, the LORD appeared to Abram, and said to him: I am God Almighty; walk before Me, and be innocent.

2. And I will make My covenant between Me and you, and will multiply you greatly.

3. And Abram fell on his face; and God talked with him, saying:

4. As for Me, my covenant is with you, and you will be the father of a multitude of nations.

5. No more will your name be called Abram, but your name will be Abraham; for I have made you the father of a multitude of nations.

6. And I will make you exceedingly fruitful, and I will make nations of you, and kings will come from you.

7. And I will establish My covenant between Me and you and your seed after you throughout their generations for an everlasting covenant, to be a God to you and to your seed after you.

8. And I will give to you, and to your seed after you, the land of your sojourning's, all the land of Canaan, for an everlasting possession; and I will be their God.

9. And God said to Abraham: And as for you, you will keep My covenant, you, and your seed after you throughout their generations.

10. This is My covenant, which you shall keep, between Me and you and your seed after you: every male among you shall be circumcised.

11. And you shall circumcise the flesh of your foreskin; and it will be a token of a covenant between Me and you.

12. And a son that is eight days old will be circumcised, every male throughout your generations, that is born in the house, or bought with money from any foreigner, that is not of your seed.

13. Those born in your house, and those bought with your money, shall be circumcised; and My covenant will be in your flesh for an everlasting covenant.

14. And the uncircumcised male who does not circumcise the flesh of his foreskin, that soul will be cut off from his people; he has broken My covenant.

15. And God said to Abraham: As for Sarai your wife, you will not call her name Sarai, but her name will be Sarah.

16. And I will bless her, and I will give you a son from her; I will bless her, and she will be a mother of nations; kings of peoples will be from her.

17. Then Abraham fell upon his face, and laughed, and said in his heart: Will a child be born to one that is a hundred years old? and will Sarah, that is ninety years old, bear?

18. And Abraham said to God: Oh, that Ishmael might live before You.

19. And God said: Sarah your wife will bear you a

son; and you will name him Isaac; and I will establish My covenant with him for an everlasting covenant for his seed after him.

20. And as for Ishmael, I have heard you; I have blessed him, and will make him fruitful, and will multiply him greatly; He will sire twelve princes, and I will make him a great nation.

21. But My covenant I will establish with Isaac, whom Sarah shall bear to you at this time next year.

22. And that was all that He said to him, and God went up from Abraham.

23. And Abraham took Ishmael his son, and all that were born in his house, and all that were bought with his money, every male among the men of Abraham's house, and circumcised the flesh of their foreskin that same day, as God had instructed him.

24. And Abraham was ninety-nine years old, when he circumcised the flesh of his foreskin.

25. And Ishmael his son was thirteen years old, when he was circumcised in the flesh of his foreskin.

26. In the same day Abraham was circumcised, and Ishmael his son.

27. And all the men of his house, those born in the house, and those bought with money of a foreigner, were circumcised with him.

Vayera

Chapter 18

1. And the LORD appeared to him by the trees of Mamre, as he sat in the tent door in the heat of the day;

2. And he looked up and saw, three men standing

opposite him; and when he saw them, he ran from the tent door to meet them, and bowed down to the earth,

3. And said: My lord, if I have found favor in your sight, do not pass by your servant.

4. Please Let me take water, and wash your feet, and you recline under the tree.

5. And I will bring a morsel of bread, and you may stay and feast your heart; after that you will go; because you have come to your servant. And they said: Do as you have said.

6. And Abraham hastened into the tent to Sarah, and said: Quickly prepare three measures of fine meal, knead it, and make cakes.

7. And Abraham ran to the herd, and picked a good and tender calf, and gave it to a boy; and he prepared it.

8. And he took cheese, and milk, and the calf which he had prepared, and set it before them; and he stood near them under the tree, and they ate.

9. And they said to him: Where is Sarah your wife? And he said: In the tent.

10. And He said: I will certainly return to you when the season returns; and, Sarah your wife will have a son. And Sarah heard in the tent door, which was behind him.

11. Now Abraham and Sarah were old, at the end of their days; and Sarah had ceased with the manner of women. -

12. And Sarah laughed within herself, saying: After I am old shall I have pleasure, my lord being old also?

13. And the LORD said to Abraham: Why did Sarah laugh, saying: Truly, will I bear a child, I am old?

14. Is anything too hard for the LORD. At this time

when this season returns, I will return to you, and Sarah will have a son.

15. Then Sarah denied it, saying: I did not laugh; for she was afraid. And He said: but you did laugh.

16. And the men rose up from there, and looked out toward Sodom; and Abraham went with them to bring them on the way.

17. And the LORD said: Will I hide from Abraham what I am doing;

18. Knowing that Abraham will become a great and mighty nation, and all the nations of the earth will be blessed by him?

19. For I know him, he commands his children and his household after him, to keep the way of the LORD, to do righteousness and justice; so, the LORD will bring upon Abraham everything He has spoken.

20. And the LORD said: The cry of Sodom and Gomorrah is great, because their sin is very grave.

21. I will go down, and see if they merit destruction according to their cry, which has come to Me; and if not, I will know.

22. And the men turned from there, and went toward Sodom; but Abraham stood before the LORD.

23. And Abraham drew near, and said: Will You sweep away the righteous with the wicked?

24. If there are fifty righteous within the city; will You destroy and not forgive the place for the fifty righteous that are there?

25. Would you debase Yourself, to slay the righteous with the wicked, that so the righteous would be like the wicked; Would you debase Yourself; will the judge of all the earth not do justice?

26. And the LORD said: If I find in Sodom fifty

righteous within the city, then I will forgive all the place because of them.

27. And Abraham answered and said: I have taken it upon myself to speak to the Lord, who am but dust and ashes.

28. If five of the fifty righteous are missing; will You destroy all the city for lack of the five? And He said: I will not destroy it, if I find forty-five.

29. And he spoke to Him yet again, and said: If forty would be found there. And He said: I will not do it for the forty's sake.

30. And he said: Please Lord do not be angry, and I will speak. If there would be thirty that are found there. And He said: I will not do it, if I find thirty there.

31. And he said: Now I have taken it upon myself to speak to the Lord. If there would be twenty found there. And He said: I will not destroy it for the twenty's sake.

32. And he said: Oh, Please Lord do not be angry, and I will speak this once more. If ten would be found there. And He said: I will not destroy it for the ten's sake.

33. And the LORD went His way, as soon as He had finished speaking to Abraham; and Abraham returned to his place.

Chapter 19

1. And the two angels came to Sodom in the evening; and Lot sat at the gate of Sodom; and Lot saw them, and rose to meet them; and he fell on his face to the ground;

2. And he said: My lords, please turn aside to your

servant's house, and stay all night, and wash your feet, and you will rise early, and go on your way. And they said: No, we will stay in the street all night.

3. And he urged them greatly; and they turned to him, and went to his house; and he made them a feast, and baked unleavened bread, and they are.

4. But before they lay down, the men of the city, even the men of Sodom, surrounded the house, young and old, all the people from every quarter.

5. And they called to Lot, and said to him: Where are the men that came in to you tonight? bring them out to us, that we may know them.

6. And Lot went out the door to them, and shut the door after him.

7. And he said: please, my brothers, do not be so wicked.

8. I have two daughters that have not known man; let me bring them to you, and you do to them as is you will; only to these men do nothing; as they have come under the shadow of my roof.

9. And they said: **Stand back**. And they said: This one came to sojourn, and he judges; now will we deal worse with you, than with them. And they pressed hard upon the man, Lot, and drew near to break the door.

10. But the men reached out their hand, and brought Lot into the house to them, and they shut the door.

11. And they struck the men that were at the door of the house with blindness, both small and great; so that they tired finding the door.

12. And the men said to Lot: Who else do you have here? son-in-law, and your sons, and your daughters, and whoever you have in the city; bring them out of the place;

13. For we will destroy this place, because the cry of it is great before the LORD; and the LORD has sent us to destroy it.

14. And Lot went out, and spoke to his sons-in-law, who had married his daughters, and said: Get up, and go away from this place; for the LORD will destroy the city. But he seemed like a joker to his sons-in-law.

15. And when the morning arose, then the angels hurried Lot, saying: Get up, take your wife, and your two daughters that are here; or you will be swept away in the iniquity of the city.

16. But he lingered; and the men grabbed hold of his hand, and of the hand of his wife, and of the hand of his two daughters; the LORD being merciful to him. And they brought him out, and set him outside the city.

17. And it came to pass, when they had brought them out, that he said: Flee for your life; do not look behind you, and do not stay in all the Plain; escape to the. mountain, or you will be swept away.

18. And Lot said to them: Please no, my lord;

19. Now, your servant has found favor in your sight, and it is great mercy, which you have shown to me in saving my life; and I cannot escape to the mountain, because evil will overtake me, and I would die.

20. Now, this city is near to flee to, and it is a little one; let me escape to it. Is it not a little one? and my soul shall live.

21. And he said to him: I have accepted you concerning this thing, that I will not overthrow the city of which you have spoken.

22. Quickly, escape there; because I cannot do

anything until you are there. So, the name of the city was called Zoar.

23. The sun had risen upon the earth when Lot came to Zoar.

24. Then the LORD caused rain upon Sodom and upon Gomorrah of brimstone and fire from the LORD out of heaven;

25. And He overturned those cities, and all the Plain, and all the inhabitants of the cities, and everything that grew upon the ground.

26. But his wife looked back from behind him, and she became a pillar of salt.

27. And Abraham got up early in the morning to the place where he had stood before the LORD.

28. And he looked out toward Sodom and Gomorrah, and toward all the land of the Plain, and saw the smoke of the land went up like the smoke of a furnace.

29. Now, when God destroyed the cities of the Plain, God remembered Abraham, and sent Lot out of the middle of the destruction, when He overturned the cities in which Lot lived.

30. And Lot went up out of Zoar, and lived in the mountain, and his two daughters with him; because he was scared to live in Zoar; and he lived in a cave, he and his two daughters.

31. And the first-born said unto the younger: Our father is old, and there is not a man on the earth to come in to us in the manner of all the earth.

32. Come, we will make our father drink wine, and we will lie with him, that we may preserve seed of our father.

33. And they made their father drink wine that night.

And the first-born went in, and lay with her father; and he did not know when she lay down, or when she arose.

34. And on the next day, that the first-born said to the younger: last night I lay with my father. We will make him drink wine tonight also; and you go in, and lie with him, that we may preserve seed of our father.

35. And they made their father drink wine that night also. And the younger arose, and lay with him; and did not know when she lay down, or when she arose.

36. So, both the daughters of Lot were with child by their father.

37. And the first-born bore a son, and named him **Moab** - he is the father of the Moabites to this day.

38. And the younger, also bore a son, and named him **Ben-ammi** - he is the father of the children of Ammon to this day.

Chapter 20

1. And Abraham journeyed from there toward the land of the South, and dwelled between Kadesh and Shur; and he sojourned in Gerar.

2. And Abraham said of Sarah his wife: She is my sister. And Abimelech king of Gerar sent for, and took Sarah.

3. But God came to Abimelech in a dream at night, and said to him: you will die, because of the woman you have taken; for she is a man's wife.

4. Now Abimelech had not come near her; and he said: Lord, will You slay even a righteous nation?

5. He said to me: She is my sister? and she, even she said: He is my brother, herself. With a pure heart and innocence hands have I done this.

6. And God said to him in the dream: I know that with a pure heart you have done this, and I also stopped you from sinning against Me. So, I did not let you touch her.

7. Now restore the man's wife; for he is a prophet, and he will pray for you, and you will live; and if you do not return her, you know that you will surely die, you, and all that is yours.

8. And Abimelech rose early in the morning, and called all his servants, and told all these things to them; and the men were very afraid.

9. Then Abimelech called Abraham, and said to him: What have you done to us? and how have I sinned against you, that you have brought to me and on my kingdom a great sin? you have done things to me that should not to be done.

10. And Abimelech said unto Abraham: What did you see, that you have done this thing?

11. And Abraham said: Because I thought: Certainly, there is no fear of God in this place; and they will kill me for my wife's sake.

12. And she is indeed my sister, the daughter of my father, but not the daughter of my mother; and so, she became my wife.

13. So, when God caused me to wander from my father's house, I said to her: This is your kindness which you will give to me; at every place where we will go, say: He is my brother.

14. And Abimelech took sheep and oxen, and men-servants and women-servants, and gave them to Abraham, and returned Sarah his wife to him.

15. And Abimelech said: See my land before you: dwell where it pleases you.

16. And to Sarah he said: See, I have given your brother a thousand pieces of silver; it is for you a covering of the eyes to all that are with you; and before all men here.

17. And Abraham prayed to God; and God healed Abimelech, and his wife, and his maid-servants; and they bore children.

18. For the LORD had closed up all the wombs of the house of Abimelech, because of Sarah Abraham's wife.

Chapter 21

1. And the LORD remembered Sarah as He had said, and the LORD did to Sarah as He had spoken.

2. And Sarah conceived, and bore Abraham a son in his old age, at the set time which God had told him.

3. And Abraham named his son that was born to him, whom Sarah bore to him, Isaac.

4. And Abraham circumcised his son Isaac when he was eight days old, as God commanded him.

5. And Abraham was one hundred years old, when his son Isaac was born to him.

6. And Sarah said: God has made laughter for me; everyone that hears will laugh because of me.

7. And she said: Who would have said to Abraham, that Sarah should give children suck? for I have borne him a son in his old age.

8. And the child grew, and was weaned. And Abraham made a great feast on the day that Isaac was weaned.

9. And Sarah saw the son of Hagar the Egyptian, whom she had borne to Abraham, making sport.

10. So, she said to Abraham: Cast out this handmaid

and her son; for the son of this handmaid will not inherit with my son, with Isaac.

11. This was upsetting in the eyes of Abraham, for the sake of his son.

12. And God said to Abraham: Do not let it be upsetting in your eyes because of the boy, and because of your handmaid; Everything that Sarah says to you, listen to her; for Isaac will be called your seed.

13. Also, I will make the son of the handmaid a nation, because he is your seed.

14. And Abraham rose early in the morning, and took bread and a bottle of water, and gave it to Hagar, putting it on her shoulder, and the child, and sent her away; and she departed, and strayed into the wilderness of Beer-sheba.

15. And the water in the bottle was gone, and she cast the child under one of the shrubs.

16. And she went, and sat her down opposite him a good way off, about a bow-shot; and she said: Let me not see the death of the child. And she sat opposite him, and lifted up her voice, and wept.

17. And God heard the voice of the boy; and the angel of God called to Hagar out of heaven, and said to her: What troubles you, Hagar? don't fear; for God has heard the voice of the boy where he is.

18. Arise, lift up the boy, and hold him fast by your hand; for I will make him a great nation.

19. And God opened her eyes, and she saw a well of water; and she went, and filled the bottle with water, and gave the boy drink.

20. And God was with the boy, and he grew; and he dwelled in the wilderness, and became an archer.

21. And he dwelled in the wilderness of Paran; and his mother took him a wife out of the land of Egypt.

22. So, at that time, Abimelech and Phicol the captain of his host spoke to Abraham, saying: God is with you in all that you do.

23. Now swear to me here by God that you will not deal falsely with me, nor with my son, nor with my son's son; but according to the kindness that I have done to you, you will do to me, and to the land where you have sojourned.

24. And Abraham said: I will swear.

25. And Abraham reprimanded Abimelech because of the well of water, which Abimelech's servants had violently taken.

26. And Abimelech said: I don't know who has done this thing; and you did not tell me, and I did not hear of it, until today.

27. And Abraham took sheep and oxen, and gave them to Abimelech; and the two made a covenant.

28. And Abraham set seven ewe-lambs of the flock by themselves.

29. And Abimelech said to Abraham: What are these seven ewe-lambs which you have set by themselves?

30. And he said: you will take these seven ewe-lambs out of my hand, that it may be a witness to me, that I dug this well.

31. So, that place was called Beer-sheba; because they both swore there.

32. So, they made a covenant at Beer-sheba; and Abimelech rose, and Phicol the captain of his host, and they returned into the land of the Philistines.

33. And Abraham planted a tamarisk-tree in Beer-sheba, and called on the name of the LORD, the

Everlasting God.

34. And Abraham sojourned in the land of the Philistines many days.

Chapter 22

1. Now, after these things, that God tested Abraham, and said to him: **Abraham**; and he said: **Here I am**.

2. And He said: Take now your son, your only son, who you love, Isaac, and go to the land of Moriah; and offer him there for a burnt-offering on one of the mountains which I will tell you.

3. And Abraham rose early in the morning, and saddled his donkey, and took two of his young men with him, and Isaac his son; and he split the wood for the burnt-offering, and rose, and went up to the place of which God had told him.

4. On the third day Abraham lifted up his eyes, and saw the place from a distance.

5. And Abraham said to his young men: You stay here with the donkey, and the boy and I will go a distance; and we will worship, and come back to you.

6. And Abraham took the wood of the burnt-offering, and laid it on Isaac his son; and he took the fire and the knife in his hand; and the two of them went together.

7. And Isaac spoke to Abraham his father, and said: **My father**. And he said: Here I am, my son. And he said: See the fire and the wood; but where is the lamb for a burnt-offering?

8. And Abraham said: God will provide the lamb for a burnt-offering Himself, my son. So, the two of them went together.

9. And they came to the place which God had told

him of; and Abraham built the altar there, and laid the wood in order, and bound Isaac his son, and laid him on the altar, upon the wood.

10. And Abraham stretched out his hand, and took the knife to slay his son.

11. And the angel of the LORD called unto him out of heaven, and said: **Abraham, Abraham**. And he said: Here am I.

12. And he said: Do not lay your hand upon the boy, don't do anything to him; for now, I know that you are a God-fearing man, seeing that you have not withheld your son, your only son, from Me.

13. And Abraham lifted up his eyes, and looked, and saw a ram behind him caught in the thicket by his horns. And Abraham went and took the ram, and offered him up for a burnt-offering instead of his son.

14. And Abraham called the name of that place Adonai-jireh; as it is said to this day: In the mount where the LORD is seen.

15. And the angel of the LORD called to Abraham a second time out of heaven,

16. And said: By Myself have I sworn, said the LORD, because you have done this thing, and have not withheld your son, your only son,

17. That in blessing I will bless you, and in multiplying I will multiply your seed as the stars of the heaven, and as the sand which is on the seashore; and your seed will possess the gate of his enemies;

18. And in your seed, all the nations of the earth will be blessed; because you have listened to My voice.

19. So, Abraham returned to his young men, and they rose and went together to Beer-sheba; and Abraham dwelt at Beer-sheba.

20. And it happened after these things, that Abraham was told: Milcah, has also borne children to your brother Nahor:

21. Uz his first-born, and Buz his brother, and Kemuel the father of Aram;

22. And Chesed, and Hazo, and Pildash, and Jidlaph, and Bethuel.

23. And Bethuel begot Rebekah; these eight did Milcah bear to Nahor, Abraham's brother.

24. And his concubine, whose name was Reumah, she also bore Tebah, and Gaham, and Tahash, and Maacah.

Chayei Sara

Chapter 23

1. And the life of Sarah was one hundred twenty-seven years; these were the years of the life of Sarah.

2. And Sarah died in Kiriat-harba - also called Hebron - in the land of Canaan; and Abraham came to mourn for Sarah, and to weep for her.

3. And Abraham rose up from before his dead, and spoke to the children of Heth, saying:

4. I am a stranger and a sojourner with you: give me a possession of a burying-place, that I may bury my dead out of my sight.

5. And the children of Heth answered Abraham, saying to him:

6. Listen, my lord: you are a mighty prince among us; in the best of our tombs bury your dead; none of us will withhold from you his tomb, but that you may bury your dead.

7. And Abraham rose up, and bowed down to the

people of the land, even to the children of Heth.

8. And he spoke with them, saying: If it is your will that I should bury my dead out of my sight, listen to me, and entreat for me to Ephron the son of Zohar,

9. That he may give me the cave of Machpelah, which he has, which is in the end of his field; let him give it to me for the full price, within your land for a possession of a burial place.

10. Now Ephron was sitting in the middle of the children of Heth; and Ephron the Hittite answered Abraham in the hearing of the children of Heth, of all that went in at the gate of his city, saying:

11. No, my lord, listen: I give you the field, and the cave that is in it, I give it you; in the presence of the sons of my people I give it to you; bury your dead.

12. And Abraham bowed down before the people of the land.

13. And he spoke to Ephron in the hearing of the people of the land, saying: But if you will hear me: I will give the price of the field; take it from me, and I will bury my dead there.

14. And Ephron answered Abraham, saying to him:

15. My lord, listen to me: a piece of land worth four hundred shekels of silver, what is that between you and me? bury your dead.

16. And Abraham listened to Ephron; and Abraham weighed out the silver to Ephron, which he had named in the hearing of the children of Heth, four hundred shekels of silver, current money with the merchant.

17. So, the field of Ephron, which was in Machpelah, which was before Mamre, the field, and the cave in it, and all the trees that were in the field, that were in the border around it, came.

18. To Abraham for a possession in the presence of the children of Heth, before all that went in at the gate of his city.

19. And after this, Abraham buried Sarah his wife in the cave of the field of Machpelah before Mamre - also called Hebron - in the land of Canaan.

20. And the field, and the cave that is in it, were given to Abraham for a possession of a burial place by the children of Heth.

Chapter 24

1. And Abraham was old, advanced in years; and the LORD had blessed Abraham in all things.

2. And Abraham said to his servant, the elder of his house, that managed all that he had: Please put your hand under my thigh.

3. And I will make you swear by the LORD, the God of heaven and the God of the earth, that you will not take a wife for my son from the daughters of the Canaanites, among whom I live.

4. But you will go to my land, and to my home, and take a wife for my son, for Isaac.

5. And the servant said to him: What if the woman will not be willing to follow me to this land; should I bring your son back to the land from where you came?

6. And Abraham said to him: You Beware that you do not bring my son back there.

7. The LORD, the God of heaven, who took me from my father's house, and from the land of my birth, and who spoke to me, and who swore to me, saying: To your seed I will give this land; He will send His angel before you, and you will take a wife for my son from there.

8. And if the woman is not willing to follow you, then you will be free from my oath; only you will not bring my son back there.

9. And the servant put his hand under his master Abraham's thigh, and swore to him concerning this matter.

10. And the servant took ten camels, of the camels of his master, and departed; having all good things of his master's in his hand; and he arose, and went to **Aram-naharaim**, to the city of Nahor.

11. And he made the camels kneel down outside the city by the water well at the time of evening, the time that women go out to draw water.

12. And he said: LORD, the God of my master Abraham, please cause it to happen today, and show kindness to my master Abraham.

13. I stand by the fountain of water; and the daughters of the men of the city come out to draw water.

14. So, let it happen, that the young woman to whom I say: Let down your pitcher, please, that I may drink; and she will say: Drink, and I will give your camels drink as well; let her be the one that You have appointed for your servant, for Isaac; and so, I will know that You have shown kindness to my master.

15. And it happened, before he had finished speaking, that, Rebekah came out, who was born to Bethuel the son of Milcah, the wife of Nahor, Abraham's brother, with her pitcher on her shoulder.

16. And the young woman had a very nice appearance, a virgin, no man had known her; and she went down to the fountain, and filled her pitcher, and came up.

17. And the servant ran to meet her, and said: Please, Give me drink, a little water from your pitcher.

18. And she said: Drink, my lord; and she quickly let down her pitcher to her hand, and gave him drink.

19. And when she had finished giving him drink, she said: I will draw for your camels as well, until they are done drinking.

20. And she quickly emptied her pitcher into the trough, and ran again unto the well to draw, and drew for all his camels.

21. And the man looked at her amazed; silently, to know if the LORD had made his journey prosperous or not.

22. So, as the camels were done drinking, that the man took a golden ring of half a shekel weight, and two bracelets for her hands of ten shekels weight of gold;

23. And said: Whose daughter, are you? tell me, please. Is there room in your father's house to accommodate us?

24. And she said to him: I am the daughter of Bethuel the son of Milcah, whom she bore to Nahor.

25. She said more to him: We have both straw and provender enough, and room to accommodate you.

26. And the man bowed his head, and prostrated himself to the LORD.

27. And he said: Blessed is the LORD, God of my master Abraham, who has not withheld His mercy and His truth toward my master; as for me, the LORD has led me to the house of the brothers of my master.

28. And the young woman ran, and told her mother's house these things.

29. And Rebekah had a brother, and his name was Laban; and Laban ran out to the man, to the fountain.
30. And when he saw the ring, and the bracelets on his sister's hands, and when he heard the words of Rebekah his sister, saying: So, the man spoke to me, so he came to the man; as he stood by the camels at the fountain.
31. And he said: Come in, you who are blessed of the LORD; why do you stand outside? I have cleared a place in the house, and made room for the camels.
32. And the man came into the house, and he unmuzzled the camels; and he gave straw and feed for the camels, and water to wash his feet and the feet of the men that were with him.
33. And there was food set before him to eat; but he said: I will not eat, until I have spoken my intent. And he said: Speak on.
34. And he said: I am Abraham's servant.
35. And the LORD has blessed my master greatly; and he has become great; and He has given him flocks and herds, and silver and gold, and menservants and maidservants, and camels and donkeys.
36. And Sarah my master's wife bore a son to my master when she was old; and to him has he given all that he has.
37. And my master made me swear, saying: You will not take a wife for my son of the daughters of the Canaanites, in whose land I live.
38. But you will go to my father's house, and to my family, and take a wife for my son.
39. And I said to my master: What if the woman will not follow me.
40. And he said to me: The LORD, I walk before, will

send His angel with you, and make good your way; and you will take a wife for my son, of my family, and of my father's house;

41. Then will you be free from my oath, when you come to my family; and if they do not give her to you, you will be free from my oath.

42. And I came today to the fountain, and said: O LORD, the God of my master Abraham, if now You make good my way which I go:

43. So, I am standing by the fountain of water; and let it be, that the young woman that comes to draw, to whom I say: Please give me a little water from your pitcher to drink;

44. And she would say to me: You drink, and I will also draw for your camels; let it be the woman whom the LORD has appointed for my master's son.

45. And before I was done speaking from my heart, Rebekah came with her pitcher on her shoulder; and she went down to the fountain, and drew. And I said to her: Please, let me drink.

46. And quickly she let down her pitcher from her shoulder, and said: Drink, and I will give your camels drink also. So, I drank, and she made the camels drink also.

47. And I asked her, and said: Whose daughter, are you? And she said: The daughter of Bethuel, Nahor's son, whom Milcah bore to him. And I put the ring on her nose, and the bracelets on her hands.

48. And I bowed my head, and prostrated myself before the LORD, and blessed the LORD, the God of my master Abraham, who had led me on the true path to take my master's brother's daughter for his son.

49. And now if you will deal kindly and truly with my master, tell me; and if not, tell me; that I may turn to the right hand, or to the left.

50. Then Laban and Bethuel answered and said: This matter comes from the LORD; we cannot say to you if it is bad or good.

51. Here, Rebekah is before you, take her, and go, and let her be your master's son's wife, as the LORD has spoken.

52. And it happened, that, when Abraham's servant heard their words, he bowed down to the earth to the LORD.

53. And the servant brought out jewels of silver, and jewels of gold, and clothes, and gave them to Rebekah; he gave also to her brother and to her mother precious things.

54. And they ate and drank, he and the men that were with him, and stayed the night; and rose in the morning, and he said: Send me away to my master.

55. And her brother and her mother said: Let the young woman stay with us a few days, or ten; after that she shall go.

56. And he said to them: Do not delay me, seeing the LORD has made good my way; send me away that I may go to my master.

57. And they said: We will call the young woman, and ask her.

58. And they called Rebekah, and said to her: Will you go with this man? And she said: I will go.

59. And they sent away Rebekah their sister, and her nurse, and Abraham's servant, and his men.

60. And they blessed Rebekah, and said to her: Our sister, may you be the mother of thousands of ten thousand, and let you seed possess the gate of those that hate them.

61. And Rebekah rose, and her maids, and they rode upon the camels, and followed the man. And the servant took Rebekah, and went his way.

62. And Isaac came from the way of Beer-lahai-roi; for he lived in the land of the South.

63. And Isaac went out to meditate in the field in the evening; and he lifted up his eyes, and saw there were camels coming.

64. And Rebekah lifted up her eyes, and when she saw Isaac, she fell from the camel.

65. And she said to the servant: What man is this that walks in the field to meet us? And the servant said: It is my master. And she took her veil, and covered herself.

66. And the servant told Isaac all the things that he had done.

67. And Isaac brought her into his mother Sarah's tent, and took Rebekah, and she became his wife; and he loved her. And Isaac was comforted for his mother.

Chapter 25

1. And Abraham took another wife, and her name was Keturah.

2. And she bore him Zimran, and Jokshan, and Medan, and Midian, and Ishbak, and Shuah.

3. And Jokshan begot Sheba, and Dedan. And the sons of Dedan were Asshurim, and Letushim, and Leummim.

4. And the sons of Midian: Ephah, and Epher, and Hanoch, and Abida, and Eldaah. All these were the children of Keturah.

5. And Abraham gave all that he had to Isaac.

6. But to the sons of the concubines, that Abraham had, Abraham gave gifts; and he sent them away from Isaac his son, while he still lived, eastward, in the east country.

7. And these are the days of the years of Abraham's life which he lived, one hundred seventy-five years.

8. And Abraham expired, and died at a good old age, an old man, and full of years; and was gathered to his people.

9. And Isaac and Ishmael his sons buried him in the cave of Machpelah, in the field of Ephron the son of Zohar the Hittite, at the face of Mamre;

10. The field which Abraham purchased of the children of Heth; there Abraham was buried, and Sarah his wife.

11. Then, after the death of Abraham, God blessed Isaac his son; and Isaac lived by Beer-lahai-roi.

12. Now these are the generations of Ishmael, Abraham's son, whom Hagar the Egyptian, Sarah's handmaid, bore to Abraham.

13. And these are the names of the sons of Ishmael, by their names, according to their generations: the first-born of Ishmael, Nebaioth; and Kedar, and Adbeel, and Mibsam,

14. And Mishma, and Dumah, and Massa;

15. Hadad, and Tema, Jetur, Naphish, and Kedem;

16. These are the sons of Ishmael, and these are their names, by their villages, and by their encampments; twelve princes according to their nations.

17. And these are the years of the life of Ishmael, one hundred thirty-seven years; and he expired and died;

and was gathered to his people.

18. And they lived from Havilah to Shur that is before Egypt, as you go toward Asshur: he settled facing his brothers.

Toldot

19. And these are the generations of Isaac, Abraham's son: Abraham begot Isaac.

20. And Isaac was forty years old when he took Rebekah, the daughter of Bethuel the Aramean, of Paddan-aram, the sister of Laban the Aramean, to be his wife.

21. And Isaac asked the LORD on behalf of his wife, because she was barren; and the LORD was asked by him, and Rebekah his wife conceived.

22. And the children struggled within her; and she said: If so, why am I like this? And she went to ask the LORD.

23. And the LORD said to her: Two nations are in your womb, and two peoples shall be separated from inside you; And the one people will be stronger than the other people; And the elder shall serve the younger.

24. And when her days to deliver were done, there were twins in her womb.

25. And the first came out ruddy, all over like a hairy coat; and they named him Esau.

26. And after that came his brother, and his hand had hold on Esau's heel; and he was named Jacob. And Isaac was sixty years old when she bore them.

27. And the boys grew; and Esau was a cunning hunter, a man of the field; and Jacob was a quiet man, dwelling in tents.

28. Now Isaac loved Esau, because he ate his venison; and Rebekah loved Jacob.

29. And Jacob cooked stew; and Esau came in from the field, and he was faint.

30. And Esau said to Jacob: Let me eat, some of this red, red stew; for I am faint. So, he was called Edom.

31. And Jacob said: First sell me your birthright.

32. And Esau said: Now, I am going to die; what good does the birthright do for me?

33. And Jacob said: Swear to me first; and he swore to him; and he sold his birthright to Jacob.

34. And Jacob gave Esau bread and stew of lentils; and he ate and drank, and got up, and went his way. So, Esau repudiated his birthright.

Chapter 26

1. And there was a famine in the land, beside the first famine that was in the days of Abraham. And Isaac went to Abimelech king of the Philistines in Gerar.

2. And the LORD appeared to him, and said: Do not go down to Egypt; live in the land which I will tell you.

3. Sojourn in this land, and I will be with you, and will bless you; for to you, and to your seed, I will give all these lands, and I will fulfill the oath which I swore to Abraham your father;

4. And I will multiply your seed as the stars of heaven, and will give to your seed all these lands; and all the nations of the earth will bless themselves by your seed;

5. Because Abraham listened to My voice, and kept My guard, My commandments, My statutes, and My laws.

6. And Isaac dwelt in Gerar.

7. And the men of the place asked him about his wife; and he said: She is my sister; for he was scared to say: My wife; So that the men of the place should not kill me for Rebekah, because she is beautiful to look upon.

8. And it happened, when he had been there a long time, that Abimelech king of the Philistines looked out at a window, and saw, and Isaac was playing with Rebekah his wife.

9. And Abimelech called Isaac, and said: She is surely your wife; and why did you say: She is my sister? And Isaac said to him: Because I said: I might die because of her.

10. And Abimelech said: What is this you have done to us? one of the people might easily have lain with your wife, and you would have brought guilt upon us.

11. And Abimelech told all the people, saying: Anyone who touches this man or his wife will be put to death.

12. And Isaac planted in that land, and found in the same year a hundred-fold; and the LORD blessed him.

13. And the man became great, and grew more and more until he became very great.

14. And he had possessions of flocks, and possessions of herds, and a great household; and the Philistines envied him.

15. Now all the wells which his father's servants dug in the days of Abraham his father, the Philistines had stopped them, and filled them with earth.

16. And Abimelech said to Isaac: Go from us; for you

are much mightier than us.

17. And Isaac departed there, and encamped in the valley of Gerar, and lived there.

18. And Isaac dug the wells of water again, which they had dug in the days of Abraham his father; for the Philistines had stopped them after the death of Abraham; and he named them after the names which his father had called them.

19. And Isaac's servants dug in the valley, and found there a well of living water.

20. And the herdsmen of Gerar argued with Isaac's herdsmen, saying: The water is ours. And he called the name of the well Esek; because they argued with him.

21. And they dug another well, and they argued for that also. And he called the name of it Sitnah.

22. And he left from there, and dug another well; and for that they did not argue. And he called the name of its Rehoboth; and he said: For now, the LORD has made room for us, and we will be fruitful in the land.

23. And he went up from there to Beer-sheba.

24. And the LORD appeared to him the same night, and said: I am the God of Abraham your father. Fear not, for I am with you, and will bless you, and multiply your seed for My servant Abraham's sake.

25. And he built an altar there, and called on the name of the LORD, and pitched his tent there; and there Isaac's servants dug a well.

26. Then Abimelech went to him from Gerar, and Ahuzzath his friend, and Phicol the captain of his guard.

27. And Isaac said unto them: Why do you come to me, seeing you hate me, and have sent me away from you?

28. And they said: We saw plainly that the LORD was with you; and we said: Let there now be an oath between us, even between us and you, and let us make a covenant with you;

29. That you will do us no harm, as we have not touched you, and as we have done to you nothing but good, and have sent you away in peace; you are now the blessed of the LORD.

30. And he made them a feast, and they ate and drank.

31. And they rose up early in the morning, and swore to one another; and Isaac sent them away, and they left him in peace.

32. And it happened the same day, that Isaac's servants came, and told him about the well which they dug, and said to him: We have found water.

33. And he called it Shibah. So, the name of the city is Beer-sheba to this day.

34. And when Esau was forty years old, he took, Judith the daughter of Beeri the Hittite, and Basemath the daughter of Elon the Hittite as wives.

35. And they were a source of bitterness of spirit to Isaac and to Rebekah.

Chapter 27

1. Now, when Isaac was old, and his eyes were dim, so that he could not see, he called Esau his elder son, and said to him: **My son**; and he said to him: Here I am.

2. And he said: See now, I am old, I don't know the day of my death.

3. So please take, your weapons, your quiver and your bow, and go out to the field, and hunt venison for me;

4. And make me tasty food, that I love, and bring it to me, so I may eat; that my soul may bless you before I die.

5. And Rebekah heard when Isaac spoke to Esau his son. And Esau went to the field to hunt for venison, and to bring it.

6. And Rebekah spoke to Jacob her son, saying: So, I heard your father speak to Esau your brother, saying:

7. Bring me venison, and make me tasty food, that I may eat, and bless you before the LORD before my death.

8. Now, my son, listen to my voice according to what I command you.

9. Go now to the flock, and fetch me from there two good young goats; and I will make them tasty food for your father, like he loves;

10. And you will bring it to your father, that he may eat, so that he may bless you before his death.

11. And Jacob said to Rebekah his mother: Now, Esau my brother is a hairy man, and I am a smooth man.

12. My father might touch me, and I will seem to him as a deceiver; and I will bring a curse upon me, and not a blessing.

13. And his mother said to him: Upon me be your curse, my son; only listen to my voice, and go fetch them to me.

14. And he went, and fetched, and brought them to his mother; and his mother made tasty food, like his father loved.

15. And Rebekah took the best clothes of Esau her elder son, which were with her in the house, and put them on Jacob her younger son.

16. And she put the skins of the young goats on his hands, and on the smooth of his neck.

17. And she gave the tasty food and the bread, which she had prepared, into the hand of her son Jacob.

18. And he came to his father, and said: My father; and he said: Here am I; who are you, my son?

19. And Jacob said to his father: I am, Esau your first-born; I have done as you instructed me. Arise, please, sit and eat of my venison, that your soul may bless me.

20. And Isaac said to his son: How is it that you have found it so quickly, my son? And he said: Because the LORD your God sent me good speed.

21. And Isaac said to Jacob: Come near, please, that I may feel you, my son, whether you are my son Esau or not.

22. And Jacob went near Isaac his father; and he felt him, and said: The voice is the voice of Jacob, but the hands are the hands of Esau.

23. And he did not recognize him, because his hands were hairy, as his brother Esau's hands; so, he blessed him.

24. And he said: Are you my son Esau? And he said: I am.

25. And he said: Bring it near, and I will eat of my son's venison, that my soul may bless you. And he brought it near, and he ate; and he brought him wine, and he drank.

26. And his father Isaac said to him: Come near now, and kiss me, my son.

27. And he came near, and kissed him. And he smelled the smell of his clothes, and blessed him, and said: See, the smell of my son is like the smell of a field which the LORD has blessed.

28. So, God give you of the dew of heaven, And of the fat places of the earth, And plenty of grain and wine.

29. Let peoples serve you, and nations bow down to you. Be lord over your brothers, and let your mother's sons bow down to you. Cursed is every one that curses you, and blessed is everyone that blesses you.

30. And it happened, that as soon as Isaac finished blessing Jacob, and Jacob had just left the presence of Isaac his father, that Esau his brother came in from his hunting.

31. And he also made tasty food, and brought it to his father; and he said to his father: Let my father arise, and eat of his son's venison, that your soul may bless me.

32. And Isaac his father said to him: Who are you? And he said: I am your son, your first-born, Esau.

33. And Isaac felt very great dread, and said: Who then is the one that has taken venison, and brought it me, and I have eaten of it, all before you came, and have blessed him? and he shall be blessed.

34. When Esau heard the words of his father, he screamed a very large and bitter scream, and said to his father: Bless me also, my father.

35. And he said: Your brother came with deception, and has taken away you're blessing.

36. And he said: Isn't he rightly named Jacob? for he has deceived me two times: he took away my birthright; and, see, now he has taken away my blessing. And he said: Have you not reserved a blessing for me?

37. And Isaac answered and said to Esau: I have made

him your lord, and all his brothers have I given to him for servants; and with grain and wine have I sustained him; and what then shall I do for you, my son?

38. And Esau said to his father: Have you only one blessing, my father? bless me also, my father. And Esau lifted up his voice, and wept.

39. And Isaac his father answered and said to him: See, of the fat places of the earth will be your dwelling, And of the dew of heaven from above;

40. And by your sword will you live, and you will serve your brother; And it will happen when you will break loose, that you will shake his yoke from off your neck.

41. And Esau hated Jacob because of the blessing his father blessed him with. And Esau said in his heart: When the days of mourning for my father are finished; then I will kill my brother Jacob.

42. It was told to Rebekah the words of Esau her elder son; and she sent and called Jacob her younger son, and said to him: Your brother Esau, is comforting himself by planning to kill you.

43. Now, my son, listen to my voice; you get up, flee to Laban my brother in Haran;

44. And stay with him a few days, until your brother's fury turns;

45. Until your brother's anger turns away from you, and he forgets what you have done to him; then I will send, and fetch you from there; why should I be lose you both in one day?

46. And Rebekah said to Isaac: I detest my life because of the daughters of Heth. If Jacob takes a wife of the daughters of Heth, like these, of the daughters of the land, what good will my life be to me?

Chapter 28

1. And Isaac called Jacob, and blessed him, and charged him, and said to him: You will not take a wife of the daughters of Canaan.

2. Arise, go to Paddan-aram, to the house of Bethuel your mother's father; and take a wife from there of the daughters of Laban your mother's brother.

3. And God Almighty bless you, and make you fruitful, and multiply you, that you may be a multitude of peoples;

4. And give the blessing of Abraham, to you, and to your seed with you; that you may inherit the land of your sojourning's, which God gave to Abraham.

5. And Isaac sent away Jacob; and he went to Paddan-aram to Laban, son of Bethuel the Aramean, the brother of Rebekah, Jacob's and Esau's mother.

6. Now Esau saw that Isaac had blessed Jacob and sent him away to Paddan-aram, to take a wife from there; and that as he blessed him, he gave him a charge, saying: You will not take a wife of the daughters of Canaan;

7. And that Jacob listened to his father and his mother, and was gone to Paddan-aram;

8. And Esau saw that the daughters of Canaan did not please Isaac his father;

9. So, Esau went to Ishmael, and took Mahalath the daughter of Ishmael Abraham's son, the sister of Nebaioth, to be his wife.

Vayetzei

10. And Jacob went out from Beer-sheba, and went

toward Haran.

11. And he came upon a place, and stayed there all night, because the sun had set; and he took one of the stones of the place, and put it under his head, and lay down in that place to sleep.

12. And he dreamed, and saw a ladder set up on the earth, and the top of it reached to heaven; and he saw the angels of God ascending and descending on it.

13. And, the LORD stood beside him, and said: I am the LORD, the God of Abraham your father, and the God of Isaac. The land where you lie, I will give it to you, and to your seed.

14. And your seed will be like the dust of the earth, and you will spread abroad to the west, and to the east, and to the north, and to the south. And in you and in your seed all the families of the earth will be blessed.

15. And, know, I am with you, and will keep you wherever you go, and will bring you back into this land; for I will not leave you, until I have done what I have spoken to you.

16. And Jacob woke from his sleep, and he said: Surely the LORD is in this place; and I did not know it.

17. And he was afraid, and said: How awesome is this place! this is none other than the house of God, and this is the gate of heaven.

18. And Jacob rose up early in the morning, and took the stone that he had put under his head, and set it up for a pillar, and poured oil on the top of it.

19. And he called the name of that place Beth-el, but the name of the city was Luz at first.

20. And Jacob made a vow, saying: If God will be

with me, and will keep me this way that I go, and will give me bread to eat, and clothes to put on,

21. So that I come back to my father's house in peace, then shall the LORD be my God,

22. And this stone, which I have set up for a pillar, will be God's house; and of all that You will give me I will give the tenth to You.

Chapter 29

1. Then Jacob moved his feet, and went to the land of the people of the east.

2. And he looked, and saw a well in the field, and, three flocks of sheep lying beside it. For out of that well they watered the flocks. And a large stone was on the mouth of the well.

3. And all the flocks gathered around; and they rolled the stone from the mouth of the well, and watered the sheep, and put the stone back on the mouth of the well in its place.

4. And Jacob said to them: My brothers, where are you from? And they said: We are of Haran.

5. And he said to them: Do you know Laban the son of Nahor? And they said: We know him.

6. And he said to them: Is he well? And they said: He is well; and, here comes his daughter Rachel with the sheep.

7. And he said: it is a long day, it is not time to gather together the cattle; water the sheep, and go and feed them.

8. And they said: We can't, until all the flocks are gathered together, and they roll the stone from the mouth of the well; then we water the sheep.

9. While he was still speaking with them, Rachel

Came with her father's sheep; for she tended them.

10. And it happened, when Jacob saw Rachel the daughter of Laban his mother's brother, and the sheep of Laban his mother's brother, that Jacob went near, and rolled the stone from the well's mouth, and watered the flock of Laban his mother's brother.

11. And Jacob kissed Rachel, and lifted up his voice, and wept.

12. And Jacob told Rachel that he was her father's brother, and that he was Rebekah's son; and she ran and told her father.

13. Then, when Laban heard the tidings of Jacob his sister's son, he ran to meet him, and embraced him, and kissed him, and brought him to his house. And he told Laban everything.

14. And Laban said to him: Surely you are my bone and my flesh. And he lived with him the for a month.

15. And Laban said to Jacob: Because you are my brother, should you serve me for free? tell me, what should your wages be?

16. Now Laban had two daughters: the name of the elder was Leah, and the name of the younger was Rachel.

17. And Leah's eyes were weak; but Rachel was of beautiful form and nice to look at.

18. And Jacob loved Rachel; and he said: I will serve you seven years for Rachel your younger daughter.

19. And Laban said: It is better that I give her to you, than that I should give her to another man; stay with me.

20. And Jacob served seven years for Rachel; and they seemed to him but a few days, for the love he had for her.

21. And Jacob said to Laban: Give me my wife, for my days are filled, that I may go in to her.

22. And Laban gathered together all the men of the place, and made a feast.

23. And it came to pass in the evening, that he took Leah his daughter, and brought her to him; and he went in to her.

24. And Laban gave Zilpah his handmaid to his daughter Leah for a handmaid.

25. And it happened in the morning that, he saw it was Leah; and he said to Laban: What did you do to me? did I not serve with you for Rachel? why then have you tricked me?

26. And Laban said: It is not done in our place, to give the younger before the first-born.

27. Fulfill the week with this one, and we will give you the other also for the service which you will give me for another seven other years.

28. And Jacob did so, and fulfilled her week; and he gave him Rachel his daughter to wife.

29. And Laban gave to Rachel his daughter Bilhah his handmaid to be her handmaid.

30. And he went in also in to Rachel, and he loved Rachel more than Leah, and served with him another seven other years.

31. And the LORD saw that Leah was hated, and he opened her womb; but Rachel was barren.

32. And Leah conceived, and bore a son, and she named him Reuben; for she said: Because the LORD has looked upon my affliction; for now, my husband will love me.

33. And she conceived again, and bore a son; and said: Because the LORD has heard that I am hated,

So, He has given me this son also. And she named him Simeon.

34. And she conceived again, and bore a son; and said: Now this time will my husband be joined to me, because I have borne him three sons. So, he was named Levi.

35. And she conceived again, and bore a son; and she said: This time will I praise the LORD. So, she named him Judah; and she stopped bearing.

Chapter 30

1. And when Rachel saw that she bore Jacob no children, Rachel envied her sister; and she said to Jacob: Give me children, or I will die.

2. And Jacob was angry with Rachel; and he said: Am I in God's place, to withhold from you the fruit of the womb?

3. And she said: See my maid Bilhah, go in to her; that she may bear upon my knees, and I may be built up through her.

4. And she gave him Bilhah her handmaid to wife; and Jacob went in to her.

5. And Bilhah conceived, and bore Jacob a son.

6. And Rachel said: God has judged me, and has also heard my voice, and has given me a son. So, she named him Dan.

7. And Bilhah Rachel's handmaid conceived again, and bore Jacob a second son.

8. And Rachel said: With God's wrestling's have I wrestled with my sister, and have prevailed. And she named him Naphtali.

9. When Leah saw that she had stopped bearing, she took Zilpah her handmaid, and gave her to Jacob to wife.

10. And Zilpah Leah's handmaid bore Jacob a son.

11. And Leah said: Fortune has come! And she named him Gad.

12. And Zilpah Leah's handmaid bore Jacob a second son.

13. And Leah said: I am Happy! for the daughters will call me happy. And she named him Asher.

14. And Reuben went in the days of wheat harvest, and found mandrakes in the field, and brought them to his mother Leah. Then Rachel said to Leah: Please give me your son's mandrakes.

15. And she said to her: Is it a small matter that you have taken away my husband? and would you take away my son's mandrakes too? And Rachel said: So, he will lie with you tonight for your son's mandrakes.

16. And Jacob came from the field in the evening, and Leah went out to meet him, and said: You must come in to me; for I have hired you with my son's mandrakes. And he lay with her that night.

17. And God listened to Leah, and she conceived, and bore Jacob a fifth son.

18. And Leah said: God has given me my wages, because I gave my handmaid to my husband. And she named him Issachar.

19. And Leah conceived again, and bore a sixth son to Jacob.

20. And Leah said: God has endowed me with a good dowry; now will my husband dwell with me, because I have borne him six sons. And she named him Zebulun.

21. And afterwards she bore a daughter, and named her Dinah.

22. And God remembered Rachel, and God listened to her, and opened her womb.

23. And she conceived, and bore a son, and said: God has taken away my reproach.

24. And she named him Joseph, saying: The LORD give me another son.

25. And it happened, when Rachel bore Joseph, that Jacob said to Laban: Send me away, that I may go to my native land, to my country.

26. Give me my wives and my children for whom I have served you, and let me go; you know my service which I have served you.

27. And Laban said to him: If I have found favour in your eyes - I have observed the signs, and the LORD has blessed me for your sake.

28. And he said: Tell me your wages, and I will give it.

29. And he said to him: You know how I have served you, and how your cattle have fared with me.

30. For it was little which you had before I came, and it has increased abundantly; and the LORD has blessed you wherever I turned. And now when will I provide for my own house as well?

31. And he said: What shall I give you? And Jacob said: You will not give me anything; if you will do this thing for me, I will feed your flock and keep it again.

32. I will pass through all your flock today, removing from there every speckled and spotted one, and every dark one among the sheep, and the spotted and speckled among the goats; and that will be my wages.

33. So, my righteousness will be a witness against me, when you will come to look over my wages that is before you: every one that is not speckled and spotted among the goats, and dark among the sheep, that is found with me will be counted stolen.

34. And Laban said: Let it be according to your words.

35. And that day he removed the he-goats that were streaked and spotted, and all the she-goats that were speckled and spotted, every one that had white in it, and all the dark ones among the sheep, and gave them into the hand of his sons.

36. And he put three days journey between himself and Jacob. And Jacob fed the rest of Laban's flocks.

37. And Jacob took rods of fresh poplar, and of the almond and of the plane-tree; and he peeled white streaks in them, making the white appear in the rods.

38. And he set the rods which he had peeled opposite the flocks in the gutters in the watering-troughs where the flocks came to drink; and they conceived when they came to drink.

39. And the flocks rutted at the sight of the rods, and the flocks bore streaked, speckled, and spotted.

40. And Jacob separated the lambs he also set the faces of the flocks toward the streaked and all the dark in the flock of Laban - and kept his own flock apart, and did not put them into Laban's flock.

41. And it happened, whenever the stronger of the flock conceived, that Jacob laid the rods before the eyes of the flock in the gutters, that they might conceive among the rods;

42. but when the flock were feeble, he did not put them in; so, the feebler were Laban's, and the stronger Jacob's.

43. And the man increased greatly, and had large

flocks, and maidservants and menservants, and camels and donkeys.

Chapter 31

1. And he heard the words of Laban's sons, saying: Jacob has taken away all that was our father's; and from that which was our father's he has taken all this wealth.

2. And Jacob saw the countenance of Laban, and, saw that it was not toward him as before.

3. And the LORD said to Jacob: Return to the land of your fathers, and to your native land; and I will be with you.

4. And Jacob sent and called Rachel and Leah to the field to his flock,

5. And said to them: I see your father's countenance, that it is not toward me as before; but the God of my father has been with me.

6. And you know that with all my power I have served your father.

7. And your father has mocked me, and changed my wages ten times; but God did not let him hurt me.

8. If he said: The speckled will be your wages; then all the flock bore speckled; and if he said: The streaked shall be your wages; then all the flock bore streaked.

9. So, God has taken away the cattle of your father, and given them to me.

10. And it happened that the flock conceived, that I lifted up my eyes, and saw in a dream, and, saw the he-goats which leaped upon the flock were streaked, speckled, and grizzled.

11. And the angel of God said to me in the dream:

Jacob; and I said: Here am I.

12. And he said: Now lift up your eyes, and see, all the he-goats which leap upon the flock are streaked, speckled, and grizzled; for I have seen all that Laban does to you.

13. I am the God of Beth-el, where you anointed a pillar, where you made a vow to Me. Now you rise, get out of this land, and return to the land of your birth.

14. And Rachel and Leah answered and said to him: Is there any portion or inheritance for us in our father's house?

15. Aren't we strangers to him? because he has sold us, and has devoured the money.

16. For all the riches which God has taken away from our father, that is ours and our children's. Now, whatever God has said to you, do it.

17. Then Jacob rose, and set his sons and his wives on the camels;

18. And he carried away all his cattle, and all his possessions that he had gathered, the cattle he had acquired, which he had gathered in Paddan-aram, to go to Isaac his father to the land of Canaan.

19. Now Laban was gone to shear his sheep. And Rachel stole the Teraphim that were her father's.

20. And Jacob outwitted Laban the Aramean, in that he did not tell him he fled.

21. So, he fled with all that he had; and he went up, and passed over the river, and set his face toward the mountain of Gilead.

22. And on the third day Laban was told that Jacob had fled.

23. And he took his brothers with him, and pursued

after him seven days journey; and he overtook him in the mountain of Gilead.

24. And God came to Laban the Aramean in a dream at night, and said to him: Beware of speaking to Jacob, either good or bad.

25. And Laban caught up with Jacob. Now Jacob had pitched his tent on the mountain; and Laban pitched with his brothers on the mountain of Gilead.

26. And Laban said to Jacob: What have you done, you snuck away, and carried my daughters away like captives of the sword?

27. Why did you flee secretly, and hide from me; and did not tell me, I would have sent you away with joy and with songs, with drum and with harp;

28. And you did not allow me to kiss my sons and my daughters? now you have behaved foolishly.

29. It is in my power to hurt you; but the God of your father spoke to me last night, saying: Beware of speaking to Jacob, either good or bad.

30. And now that you are gone, because long for your father's house, why have you stolen my gods?

31. And Jacob answered and said to Laban: Because I was afraid; for I said: you may take your daughters from me by force.

32. Whoever you find your gods with, will not live; before our brothers determine what is yours, I have, and take it. For Jacob did not know that Rachel had stolen them.

33. And Laban went into Jacob's tent, and into Leah's tent, and into the tent of the two maid-servants; but he did not find them. And he went out of Leah's tent, and entered into Rachel's tent.

34. Now Rachel had taken the teraphim, and put them

in the saddle of the camel, and sat upon them. And Laban felt all about the tent, but did not find them.

35. And she said to her father: Do not be angry my lord, that I cannot rise up before you; for the manner of women is upon me. And he searched, but did not find the teraphim.

36. And Jacob was angry, and fought with Laban. And Jacob answered and said to Laban: What is my crime? what is my sin, that you have hotly pursued after me?

37. You have felt about all that is mine, what have you found of all your household possessions? Set it here before my brothers and your brothers, that they may judge between the two of us.

38. These twenty years have I been with you; your ewes and your she-goats have not lost their young, and I have not eaten the rams of your flocks.

39. Anything torn by beasts I did not bring to your house; I bore the loss of it; from my hand did you require it, whether stolen by day or stolen by night.

40. So, in the day the drought consumed me, and the frost by night; and my sleep fled from my eyes.

41. For twenty years have I been in your house: I served you fourteen years for your two daughters, and six years for your flock; and you have changed my wages ten times.

42. If the God of my father, the God of Abraham, and the Fear of Isaac, had not been on my side, surely you would have sent me away empty. God has seen my affliction and the labour of my hands, and gave judgment last night.

43. And Laban answered and said to Jacob: The daughters are my daughters, and the children are my children, and the flocks are my flocks, and all that you see is mine; and what can I do today for my daughters, or for their children whom they have borne?

44. And now come, let us make a covenant, you and I; and let it be a witness between you and me.

45. And Jacob took a stone, and set it up for a pillar.

46. And Jacob said to his brothers: Gather stones; and they took stones, and made a pile. And they ate there by the pile.

47. And Laban called it **Jegar-sahadutha**; but Jacob called it **Galeed**.

48. And Laban said: This heap is witness between you and me today. So, it was named Galeed;

49. And Mizpah, for he said: The LORD watch between you and me, when we are apart from one another.

50. If you will afflict my daughters, and if you will take wives beside my daughters, no man being with us; see, God is witness between me and you.

51. And Laban said to Jacob: See this pile, and see the pillar, which I have set up between you and me.

52. This pile is witness, and the pillar is witness, that I will not pass over this pile to you, and that you will not pass over this pile and this pillar to me, for harm.

53. The God of Abraham, and the God of Nahor, the God of their father, judge between us. And Jacob swore by the Fear of his father Isaac.

54. And Jacob offered a sacrifice in the mountain, and called his brothers to eat bread; and they did eat bread, and stayed all night in the mountain.

Chapter 32

1. And early in the morning Laban rose up, and

kissed his sons and his daughters, and blessed them. And Laban departed, and returned to his place.

2. And Jacob went on his way, and the angels of God met him.

3. And Jacob said when he saw them: This is God's camp. And he named the place Mahanaim.

Vayishlach

4. And Jacob sent messengers before him to Esau his brother to the land of Seir, the field of Edom.

5. And he commanded them, saying: You will say to my lord Esau: Jacob your servant says: I have sojourned with Laban, and stayed until now.

6. And I have oxen, and donkeys and flocks, and menservants and maidservants; and I have sent to tell my lord, that I may find favor in your eyes.

7. And the messengers returned to Jacob, saying: We came to your brother Esau, and he comes to meet you, and four hundred men with him.

8. Then Jacob was very afraid and was distressed. And he divided the people that were with him, and the flocks, and the herds, and the camels, into two camps.

9. And he said: If Esau comes to one camp, and destroys it, then the camp that is left will escape.

10. And Jacob said: O God of my father Abraham, and God of my father Isaac, O LORD, who said to me: Return to your country, and to your brothers, and I will do you good;

11. I am not worthy of all the mercies, and of all the truth, which You have shown to Your servant; for with my staff, I passed over this Jordan; and now I have become two camps.

12. Deliver me, please, from the hand of my brother, from the hand of Esau; I fear him, that he will come and kill me, the mother with the children.

13. And You said: I will do you good, and make your seed as the sand of the sea, which cannot be numbered for multitude.

14. And he stayed there that night; and took of what he had with him a present for Esau his brother:

15. Two hundred she-goats and twenty he-goats, two hundred ewes, and twenty rams,

16. Thirty milk camels and their colts, forty cattle and ten bulls, twenty she-donkeys and ten foals.

17. And he gave them to the hand of his servants, every drove by itself; and said to his servants: Pass before me, and put a space between drove and drove.

18. And he commanded the first, saying: When Esau my brother meets you, and asks you, saying: Who are you? and where do you go? and whose are these before you?

19. Then you will say: They are your servant, Jacob's; it is a present sent to my lord, to Esau; and he is behind us.

20. And he commanded also the second, and the third, and all that followed the droves, saying: These are the words you will speak to Esau, when you find him;

21. And you will say: Also, your servant Jacob is behind us. For he said: I will appease him with the present that goes before me, and afterward I will see his face; maybe he will accept me.

22. So, the present passed before him; and he himself stayed that night in the camp.

23. And he rose up that night, and took his two wives, and his two handmaids, and his eleven children, and passed over the ford of the Jabbok.

24. And he took them, and sent them over the stream, and sent over all which he had.

25. And Jacob was left alone; and there wrestled a man, with him, until the breaking of the day.

26. And when he saw that he did not prevail against him, he touched the hollow of his thigh; and the hollow of Jacob's thigh was injured, as he wrestled with him.

27. And he said: Let me go, for the day breaks. And he said: I will not let you go, until you bless me.

28. And he said to him: What is your name? And he said: **Jacob**.

29. And he said: Your name will no longer be Jacob, but **Israel**; for you have striven with God and with men, and have prevailed.

30. And Jacob asked him, and said: Please tell me your name. And he said: Why is it that you ask my name? And he blessed him there.

31. And Jacob called the name of the place Peniel: for I have seen God face to face, and my soul is preserved.

32. And the sun rose upon him as he passed over Peniel, and he limped upon his thigh.

33. So, the children of Israel do not eat the sinew of the thigh-vein which is on the hollow of the thigh, to this day; because he touched the hollow of Jacob's thigh, in the sinew of the thigh-vein.

Chapter 33

1. And Jacob lifted up his eyes and looked, and Esau came, and with him four hundred men. And he divided the children to Leah, and to Rachel, and to the two handmaids.

2. And he put the handmaids and their children first, and Leah and her children after, and Rachel and Joseph behind.

3. And he himself went in front them, and bowed to the ground seven times, until he came near to his brother.

4. And Esau ran to meet him, and embraced him, and fell on his neck, and kissed him; and they wept.

5. And he lifted up his eyes, and saw the women and the children; and said: Who are these with you? And he said: The children that God has graciously given your servant.

6. Then the handmaids came near, they and their children, and they bowed down.

7. And Leah also and her children came near, and bowed down; and after came Joseph near and Rachel, and they bowed down.

8. And he said: What do you mean by all this camp which I met? And he said: To find favour in the eyes of my lord.

9. And Esau said: I have enough; my brother, let what you have be yours.

10. And Jacob said: No, please, if I have found favour in your eyes, then receive my presents at my hand; because seeing your face, is like seeing the face of God, and you were pleased with me.

11. Please take the gift that is brought to you; because God has dealt graciously with me, and because I have enough. And he urged him, and he took it.

12. And he said: Let us take our journey, and let us go, and I will go before you.

13. And he said to him: My lord knows that the

children are young, and that the flocks and herds with young are in my care; and if I overdrive them in one day, all the flocks will die.

14. Please, let my lord, go before his servant; and I will journey on gently, according to the pace of the cattle that are before me and according to the pace of the children, until I come to my lord in Seir.

15. And Esau said: Let me now leave with you some of the men that are with me. And he said: for what purpose? let me find favour in the eyes of my lord.

16. So, Esau returned that day on his way unto Seir.

17. And Jacob journeyed to Succoth, and built him a house, and made booths for his cattle. So, the name of the place is called Succoth.

18. And Jacob came in peace to the city of Shechem, which is in the land of Canaan, when he came from Paddan-aram; and encamped near the city.

19. And he purchased the ground, where he pitched his tent, at the hand of the children of Hamor, Shechem's father, for a hundred pieces of money.

20. And he erected an altar there, and called it El-elohe-Israel.

Chapter 34

1. And Dinah the daughter of Leah, whom she had borne to Jacob, went out to see the daughters of the land.

2. And Shechem the son of Hamor the Hivite, the prince of the land, saw her; and he took her, and lay with her, and humbled her.

3. And his soul cleaved to Dinah the daughter of Jacob, and he loved the young woman, and spoke words to her heart.

4. And Shechem spoke to his father Hamor, saying: Get me this young woman for a wife.

5. Now Jacob heard that he had defiled Dinah his daughter; and his sons were with his cattle in the field; and Jacob was silent until they came.

6. And Hamor the father of Shechem went out to Jacob to speak with him.

7. And the sons of Jacob came in from the field when they heard it; and the men were grieved, and they were very angry, because he had performed a vile deed in Israel in lying with Jacob's daughter; which should not to be done.

8. And Hamor spoke with them, saying - The soul of my son Shechem longs for your daughter. Please give her to him as a wife.

9. And make marriages with us; give your daughters to us, and take our daughters to you.

10. And you will live with us; and the land will be before you; live and trade in it, and procure possessions in it.

11. And Shechem said to her father and to her brothers: Let me find favor in your eyes, and what you will say, I will give.

12. Ask me a large dowry and gift, and I will give what you say; but give me the young woman to wife.

13. And the sons of Jacob answered Shechem and Hamor his father with guile, because he had defiled Dinah their sister,

14. And said to them: We cannot do this thing, to give our sister to one that is uncircumcised; for that is a disgrace to us.

15. We will consent only on this condition: if you will be as we are, that every male is circumcised;

16. Then will we give our daughters to you, and we will take your daughters to us, and we will dwell with you, and we will become one people.

17. But if you will not listen to us, to be circumcised; then will we take our daughter, and we will go.

18. And their words pleased Hamor, and Shechem Hamor's son.

19. And the young man did not wait to do this, because he delighted in Jacob's daughter. And he was honored above all the house of his father.

20. And Hamor and Shechem his son came to the gate of their city, and spoke with the men of their city, saying:

21. These men are peaceable; so, let them live in the land, and trade in it; for, the land is large enough for them; let us take their daughters to us for wives, and let us give them our daughters.

22. Only on this condition will the men consent to dwell with us, to become one people, if every male among us is circumcised, as they are circumcised.

23. Won't their cattle and their substance and all their beasts be ours? only let us consent to them, and they will dwell with us.

24. All that went out to the gate of his city listened to Hamor and to Shechem his son; and every male was circumcised, all that went out to the gate of his city.

25. And it happened on the third day, when they were in pain, that two of the sons of Jacob, Simeon and Levi, Dinah's brothers, each man took his sword, and came upon the city by surprise, and killed all the males.

26. And they killed Hamor and Shechem his son with the edge of the sword, and took Dinah out of

Shechem's house, and left.

27. The sons of Jacob came upon the slain, and ransacked the city, because they had defiled their sister.

28. They took their flocks and their herds and their donkeys, and what was in the city and what was in the field;

29. And all their wealth, and all their small children and their wives, they took captive and spoiled, and everything that was in the house.

30. And Jacob said to Simeon and Levi: You have troubled me, to make me detestable to the inhabitants of the land, even to the Canaanites and the Perizzites; and, being few in number, they will gather themselves together against me and kill me; and I will be destroyed, me and my house.

31. And they said: Should he make our sister a whore?

Chapter 35

1. And God said to Jacob: Get up and go to Beth-el, and live there; and make an altar to God, who appeared to you when you fled from the face of Esau your brother.

2. Then Jacob said to his household, and to all that were with him: Put away the strange gods that are among you, and purify yourselves, and change your clothes;

3. And let us rise, and go to Beth-el; and I will make an altar to God, who answered me in the day of my distress, and was with me where I went.

4. And they gave all the foreign gods which were in their hand to Jacob, and the rings which were in their ears; and Jacob hid them under the terebinth which was by Shechem.

5. And they journeyed; and a terror of God was upon the cities that were around them, and they did not pursue after the sons of Jacob.

6. So, Jacob came to Luz, which is in the land of Canaan - also called Beth-el - he and all the people that were with him.

7. And he built an altar there, and called the place El-beth-el, because God was revealed to him there, when he fled from the face of his brother.

8. And Deborah, Rebekah's nurse died, and she was buried below Beth-el under the oak; and it was named Allon-bacuth.

9. And God appeared to Jacob again, when he came from Paddan-aram, and blessed him.

10. And God said to him: Your name is Jacob: your name will not be Jacob any more, but Israel will be your name; and He named him Israel.

11. And God said to him: I am God Almighty. Be fruitful and multiply; a nation and a company of nations will be from you, and kings will come out of your loins;

12. And the land which I gave to Abraham and Isaac, I will give it to you, and to your seed after you I will give the land.

13. And God went up from him in the place where He spoke with him.

14. And Jacob set up a pillar in the place where He spoke with him, a pillar of stone, and he poured out a drink-offering on it, and poured oil on it.

15. And Jacob named the place where God spoke with him, Beth-el.

16. And they journeyed from Beth-el; and there was still some way to come to Ephrath; and Rachel gave birth, and she had hard labour.

17. And it happened, when she was in hard labour, that the midwife said to her: Don't fear; for this also is a son.

18. And happened, as her soul was departing - for she died - that she called his name Ben-oni; but his father called him Benjamin.

19. And Rachel died, and was buried in the way to Ephrath - also called Beth-lehem.

20. And Jacob set up a pillar on her grave; it is called the pillar of Rachel's grave to this day.

21. And Israel journeyed, and spread his tent beyond Migdal-eder.

22. And it happened, while Israel lived in that land, that Reuben went and lay with Bilhah his father's concubine; and Israel heard of it. Now the sons of Jacob were twelve:

23. The sons of Leah: Reuben, Jacob's firstborn, and Simeon, and Levi, and Judah, and Issachar, and Zebulun;

24. The sons of Rachel: Joseph and Benjamin;

25. And the sons of Bilhah, Rachel's handmaid: Dan and Naphtali;

26. And the sons of Zilpah, Leah's handmaid: Gad and Asher. These are the sons of Jacob, that were born to him in Paddan-aram.

27. And Jacob came to Isaac his father to Mamre, to Kiriatharba - also called Hebron - where Abraham and Isaac sojourned.

28. And the days of Isaac were a hundred eighty years.

29. And Isaac expired, and died, and was gathered to his people, old and advanced in years; and Esau and Jacob his sons buried him.

Chapter 36

1. Now these are the generations of Esau - also called Edom.

2. Esau took his wives of the daughters of Canaan; Adah the daughter of Elon the Hittite, and Oholibamah the daughter of Anah, the daughter of Zibeon the Hivite,

3. And Basemath Ishmael's daughter, sister of Nebaioth.

4. And Adah bore to Esau Eliphaz; and Basemath bore Reuel;

5. And Oholibamah bore Jeush, and Jalam, and Korah. These are the sons of Esau, that were born to him in the land of Canaan.

6. And Esau took his wives, and his sons, and his daughters, and all the souls of his house, and his cattle, and all his beasts, and all his possessions, which he had gathered in the land of Canaan; and went into a land away from his brother Jacob.

7. For their substance was too great for them to live together; and the land of their sojournings could not bear them because of their cattle.

8. And Esau lived in the mountain-land of Seir - Esau is Edom.

9. And these are the generations of Esau the father of the Edomites in the mountain-land of Seir.

10. These are the names of Esau's sons: Eliphaz the son of Adah the wife of Esau, Reuel the son of Basemath the wife of Esau.

11. And the sons of Eliphaz were Teman, Omar, Zepho, and Gatam, and Kenaz.

12. And Timna was concubine to Eliphaz Esau's son; and she bore to Eliphaz Amalek. These are the sons of Adah Esau's wife.

13. And these are the sons of Reuel: Nahath, and Zerah, Shammah, and Mizzah. These were the sons of Basemath Esau's wife.

14. And these were the sons of Oholibamah the daughter of Anah, the daughter of Zibeon, Esau's wife; and she bore to Esau Jeush, and Jalam, and Korah.

15. These are the chiefs of the sons of Esau: the sons of Eliphaz the first-born of Esau: the chief of Teman, the chief of Omar, the chief of Zepho, the chief of Kenaz,

16. The chief of Korah, the chief of Gatam, the chief of Amalek. These are the chiefs that came of Eliphaz in the land of Edom. These are the sons of Adah.

17. And these are the sons of Reuel Esau's son: the chief of Nahath, the chief of Zerah, the chief of Shammah, the chief of Mizzah. These are the chiefs that came of Reuel in the land of Edom. These are the sons of Basemath Esau's wife.

18. And these are the sons of Oholibamah Esau's wife: the chief of Jeush, the chief of Jalam, the chief of Korah. These are the chiefs that came of Oholibamah the daughter of Anah, Esau's wife.

19. These are the sons of Esau, and these are their chiefs; also called Edom.

20. These are the sons of Seir the Horite, the inhabitants of the land: Lotan and Shobal and Zibeon and Anah,

21. And Dishon and Ezer and Dishan. These are the chiefs that came of the Horites, the children of Seir in the land of Edom.

22. And the children of Lotan were Hori and Hemam; and Lotan's sister was Timna.

23. And these are the children of Shobal: Alvan and Manahath and Ebal, Shepho and Onam.

24. And these are the children of Zibeon: Aiah and Anah - this is Anah who found the hot springs in the wilderness, as he fed the donkeys of Zibeon his father.

25. And these are the children of Anah: Dishon and Oholibamah the daughter of Anah.

26. And these are the children of Dishon: Hemdan and Eshban and Ithran and Cheran.

27. These are the children of Ezer: Bilhan and Zaavan and Akan.

28. These are the children of Dishan: Uz and Aran.

29. These are the chiefs that came of the Horites: the chief of Lotan, the chief of Shobal, the chief of Zibeon, the chief of Anah,

30. The chief of Dishon, the chief of Ezer, the chief of Dishan. These are the chiefs that came of the Horites, according to their chiefs in the land of Seir.

31. And these are the kings that reigned in the land of Edom, before any king reigned over the children of Israel.

32. And Bela the son of Beor reigned in Edom; and the name of his city was Dinhabah.

33. And Bela died, and Jobab the son of Zerah of Bozrah reigned in his stead.

34. And Jobab died, and Husham of the land of the Temanites reigned in his stead.

35. And Husham died, and Hadad the son of Bedad, who killed Midian in the field of Moab, reigned in his place; and the name of his city was Avith.

36. And Hadad died, and Samlah of Masrekah reigned in his place.

37. And Samlah died, and Shaul of Rehoboth by the River reigned in his place.

38. And Shaul died, and Baal-hanan the son of Achbor reigned in his place.

39. And Baal-hanan the son of Achbor died, and Hadar reigned in his place; and the name of the city was Pau; and his wife's name was Mehetabel, the daughter of Matred, the daughter of Me-zahab.

40. And these are the names of the chiefs that came of Esau, according to their families, after their places, by their names: the chief of Timna, the chief of Alvah, the chief of Jetheth;

41. The chief of Oholibamah, the chief of Elah, the chief of Pinon;

42. The chief of Kenaz, the chief of Teman, the chief of Mibzar;

43. The chief of Magdiel, the chief of Iram. These are the chiefs of Edom, according to their habitations in the land of their possession. This is Esau the father of the Edomites.

Vayeshev

Chapter 37

1. And Jacob lived in the land of his father's sojournings, in the land of Canaan.

2. These are the generations of Jacob. Joseph, being seventeen years old, was feeding the flock with his brothers, being still a young man with the sons of Bilhah, and with the sons of Zilpah, his father's wives; and Joseph brought evil report of them unto their father.

3. Now Israel loved Joseph more than all his children, because he was the son of his old age; and he made him a coat of many colors.

4. And when his brothers saw that their father loved him more than all his brothers, they hated him, and could not speak peaceably to him.

5. And Joseph dreamed a dream, and he told it to his brothers; and they hated him even more.

6. And he said to them: Please listen to, this dream which I have dreamed:

7. We were binding sheaves in the field, and, my sheaf rose, and stood upright; and, your sheaves circled, and bowed down to my sheaf.

8. And his brothers said to him: Will you reign over us? or will you have power over us? And they hated him even more because of his dreams, and because of his words.

9. And he dreamed another dream, and told it to his brothers, and said: I have dreamed another dream: and, the sun and the moon and eleven stars bowed down to me.

10. And he told it to his father, and to his brothers; and his father rebuked him, and said to him: What is this dream that you have dreamed? Will your mother and your brothers and I come to bow down to you, to the earth?

11. And his brothers envied him; but his father kept the dream in mind.

12. And his brothers went to feed their father's flock in Shechem.

13. And Israel said to Joseph: Don't your brothers feed the flock in Shechem? come, and I will send you to them. And he said to him: Here am I.

14. And he said to him: Go now, see if it is well with your brothers, and well with the flock; and bring me back word. So, he sent him out of the vale of Hebron, and he came to Shechem.

15. And a man found him, and, he was wandering in the field. And the man asked him, saying: What do you seek?

16. And he said: I seek my brothers. Please, tell me where they are feeding the flock.

17. And the man said: They have left; I heard them say: Let us go to Dothan. And Joseph went after his brothers, and found them in Dothan.

18. And they saw him afar off, and before he came near to them, they conspired against him to kill him.

19. And they said one to another: Look, this dreamer comes.

20. Come now, and let's kill him, and throw him into one of the pits, and we will say: An evil beast has devoured him; and we will see what will come of his dreams.

21. And Reuben heard it, and delivered him out of their hand; and said: Let us not take his life.

22. And Reuben said to them: Shed no blood; throw him into this pit that is in the wilderness, but lay no hand upon him, that he might deliver him out of their hand, to restore him to his father.

23. And it happened, when Joseph was come to his brothers, that they stripped Joseph of his coat, the coat of many colors that was on him;

24. And they took him, and cast him into the pit - and the pit was empty, there was no water in it.

25. And they sat down to eat bread; and they lifted up their eyes and looked, and saw, a caravan of Ishmaelites came from Gilead, with their camels' bearing spices and balm and ladanum, going to carry it down to Egypt.

26. And Judah said to his brethren: What profit is it if we slay our brother and conceal his blood?

27. Come, and let us sell him to the Ishmaelites, and don't let our hand be upon him; for he is our brother, our flesh. And his brothers listened to him.

28. And there passed by Midianites, merchantmen; and they drew and lifted up Joseph out of the pit, and sold Joseph to the Ishmaelites for twenty shekels of silver. And they brought Joseph into Egypt.

29. And Reuben returned to the pit; and saw Joseph was not in the pit; and he ripped his clothes.

30. And he returned to his brothers, and said: The child is gone; and as for me, where will I go?

31. And they took Joseph's coat, and killed a he-goat, and dipped the coat in the blood;

32. And they sent the coat of many colours, and they brought it to their father; and said: We have found this. Do you know if it is your son's coat or not.

33. And he knew it, and said: It is my son's coat; an evil beast has devoured him; Joseph is without doubt torn in pieces.

34. And Jacob ripped his clothes, and put sackcloth upon his loins, and mourned for his son many days.

35. And all his sons and all his daughters rose up to comfort him; but he refused to be comforted; and he said: **No** I will go to the grave mourning for my son. And his father wept for him.

36. And the Midianites sold him into Egypt to Potiphar, an officer of Pharaoh's, the captain of the guard.

Chapter 38

1. And it happened at that time, that Judah went down from his brothers, and turned to an Adullamite man, whose name was Hirah.

2. And Judah saw a daughter of a Canaanite whose name was Shua; and he took her, and went in to her.

3. And she conceived, and bore a son; and he named him Er.

4. And she conceived again, and bore a son; and she named him Onan.

5. And she bore another son, and named him Shelah; and he was at Chezib, when she bore him.

6. And Judah took a wife for Er his first-born, and her name was Tamar.

7. And Er, Judah's first-born, was wicked in the sight of the LORD; and the LORD killed him.

8. And Judah said to Onan: Go in to your brother's wife, and perform the duty of a husband's brother to her, and raise up descendants for your brother.

9. And Onan knew that the descendants would not be his; and it happened when he went in to his brother's wife, that he spilled it on the ground, so he would not give seed to his brother.

10. And what he did was evil in the sight of the LORD; and He killed him also.

11. Then Judah said to Tamar his daughter-in-law: Remain a widow in your father's house, until Shelah my son is grown up; for he said: he might also die, like his brothers. And Tamar went and lived in her father's house.

12. And in time Shua's daughter, the wife of Judah, died; and Judah was comforted, and went up unto his sheep-shearers to Timnah, he and his friend Hirah the Adullamite.

13. And Tamar was told, saying: your father-in-law goes up to Timnah to shear his sheep.

14. And she took off the garments of her widowhood, and covered herself with her veil, and wrapped herself, and sat in the entrance of Enaim, which is by the way to Timnah; for she saw that Shelah was grown up, and she was not given to him to wife.

15. When Judah saw her, he thought she was a harlot; for she had covered her face.

16. And he turned to her, and said: Please let me come in to you; for he did not know that she was his daughter-in-law. And she said: What will you give me, that you may come in to me?

17. And he said: I will send you a kid of the goats from the flock. And she said: Will you give me a pledge, till you send it?

18. And he said: What pledge will I give you? And she said: Your signet and your cord, and your staff that is in your hand. And he gave them to her, and came in to her, and she conceived by him.

19. And she rose, and went away, and took off her veil, and put on the garments of her widowhood.

20. And Judah sent the kid of the goats by the hand of his friend the Adullamite, to receive the pledge from the woman's hand; but he did not find her.

21. Then he asked the men of her place, saying:

Where is the harlot, that was at Enaim by the wayside? And they said: There has been no harlot here.

22. And he returned to Judah, and said: I have not found her; and also, the men of the place said: There has been no harlot here.

23. And Judah said: Let her take it, or we might be put to shame, I sent the kid, and you have not found her.

24. And it happened about three months after, that it was told to Judah, saying: Tamar your daughter-in-law has played the harlot; and more, she is with child by harlotry. And Judah said: Bring her out, and let her be burnt.

25. When she was brought out, she sent to her father-in-law, saying: I am with child, by the man whose these are; and she said: Please, Determine, whose these are, the signet, and the cords, and the staff.

26. And Judah acknowledged them, and said: She is more righteous than I; Since I did not give her to Shelah my son. And he did not know her again.

27. And it happened in the time of her childbirth, that, twins were in her womb.

28. And it happened, when she gave birth, that one put out a hand; and the midwife took and bound upon his hand a scarlet thread, saying: This came out first.

29. And it happened, as he drew back his hand, that, his brother came out; and she said: Why have you made a breach for yourself? So, he was named Perez.

30. And afterward his brother that had the scarlet thread upon his hand came out; and his name was called Zerah.

Chapter 39

1. And Joseph was brought down to Egypt; and Potiphar, an officer of Pharaoh's, the captain of the guard, an Egyptian, bought him from the hand of the Ishmaelites, who had brought him there.

2. And the LORD was with Joseph, and he was a prosperous man; and he was in the house of his master the Egyptian.

3. And his master saw that the LORD was with him, and that the LORD made everything he did successful.

4. And Joseph found favor in his sight, and he served to him. And he appointed him overseer over his house, and all that he had he put into his hand.

5. And it happened from the time that he appointed him overseer in his house, and over all that he had, that the LORD blessed the Egyptian's house for Joseph's sake; and the blessing of the LORD was on all that he had, in the house and in the field.

6. And he left all that he had in Joseph's hand; and, having him, he knew nothing except the bread he ate. And Joseph had a beautiful form and handsome face.

7. And it happened after these things, that his master's wife cast her eyes upon Joseph; and she said: Lie with me.

8. But he refused, and said to his master's wife: My master, having me, does not know what is in the house, and he has put all that he has into my hand;

9. He is not greater in this house than I; he has not kept back anything from me but you, because you are his wife. How then can I do this great wickedness, and sin against God?

10. And it happened, as she spoke to Joseph Day by

day, that he did not listen to her, to lie with her, or to be with her.

11. And it happened one day, when he went into the house to do his work, and there were none of the men of the house there,

12. That she caught him by his garment, saying: Lie with me. And he left his garment in her hand, and fled, and got him out.

13. And it happened, when she saw that he had left his garment in her hand, and had fled,

14. That she called to the men of her house, and spoke to them, saying: See, he has brought in a Hebrew to us to mock us; he came in to me to lie with me, and I cried with a loud voice.

15. And it happened, when he heard that I lifted up my voice and cried, that he left his garment with me, and fled, and went out.

16. And she kept his garment by her, until his master came home.

17. And she spoke to him, saying: The Hebrew servant, who you have brought to us, came in to me to mock me.

18. And it happened, as I lifted up my voice and cried, that he left his garment by me, and fled.

19. And it happened, when his master heard the words of his wife, which she spoke to him, saying: This is what your servant did to me; and his anger was kindled.

20. And Joseph's master took him, and put him into prison, the place where the king's prisoners were kept; and he was there in the prison.

21. But the LORD was with Joseph, and showed kindness to him, and gave him favor in the sight of the keeper of the prison.

22. And the keeper of the prison committed to Joseph's hand all the prisoners that were in the prison; and whatever they did there, he did it.

23. The keeper of the prison did not oversee anything that was under his hand, because the LORD was with him; and all that he did, the LORD made prosper.

Chapter 40

1. And it happened after this, that the butler of the king of Egypt and his baker offended their lord the king of Egypt.

2. And Pharaoh was angry with his two officers, the chief of the butlers, and the chief of the bakers.

3. And he put them in custody in the house of the captain of the guard, into the prison, the place where Joseph was imprisoned.

4. And the captain of the guard charged Joseph to be with them, and he served them; and they continued a season in the prison.

5. And they dreamed a dream both of them, each man his dream, in one night, each man puzzled over the interpretation of his dream, the butler and the baker of the king of Egypt, who were bound in the prison.

6. And Joseph came to them in the morning, and saw them, and, they were sad.

7. And he asked Pharaoh's officers that were with him in the ward of his master's house, saying: Why do you look so sad today?

8. And they said to him: We have dreamed a dream, and there is no one that can interpret it. And Joseph said to them: Don't interpretations belong to God? Please tell me.

9. And the chief butler told his dream to Joseph, and said to him: In my dream, I saw a vine was before me;

10. And in the vine were three branches; and as it was budding, its blossoms reached out, and the clusters on it produced ripe grapes,

11. And Pharaoh's cup was in my hand; and I took the grapes, and pressed them into Pharaoh's cup, and I gave the cup into Pharaoh's hand.

12. And Joseph said to him: This is the interpretation of it: the three branches are three days;

13. In three days, Pharaoh will lift up your head, and restore you to your office; and you will give Pharaoh's cup into his hand, as it was when you were his butler.

14. But remember me when it is well with you, and please show kindness to me, and make mention of me to Pharaoh, and bring me out of this house.

15. For I was stolen away out of the land of the Hebrews; and here I have done nothing that they should put me into the dungeon.

16. When the chief baker saw that the interpretation was good, he said to Joseph: I also had a dream, and, I saw three baskets of white bread were on my head;

17. And in the top basket there were of all kinds of baked food for Pharaoh; and the birds ate them out of the basket on my head.

18. And Joseph answered and said: This is the interpretation of it: the three baskets are three days;

19. In three days, Pharaoh will lift your head off of you, and will hang you on a tree; and the birds will eat your flesh off you.

20. And it happened the third day, which was Pharaoh's birthday, that he made a feast for all his servants; and he lifted up the head of the chief butler and the head of the chief baker among his servants.

21. And he restored the chief butler to his butlership; and he gave the cup into Pharaoh's hand.

22. But he hanged the chief baker, as Joseph had interpreted to them.

23. Although, the chief butler did not remember Joseph, but forgot him.

Miketz

Chapter 41

1. And it happened at the end of two full years, that Pharaoh dreamed: he stood by the river.

2. And seven cows came out of the river, they had a handsome appearance and healthy flesh; and they fed in the reed-grass.

3. And seven other cows came up after them out of the river, they had ill appearance and gaunt flesh; and they stood by the other cows on the edge of the river.

4. And the ill appearing and gaunt fleshed cows ate up the seven handsome and fat cows. So, Pharaoh awoke.

5. And he slept and dreamed a second time: and seven ears of corn grew on one stalk, healthy and good.

6. And, seven ears, thin and blasted with the east wind, sprung up after them.

7. And the thin ears swallowed up the seven healthy and full ears. And Pharaoh awoke, and saw it was a dream.

8. And it happened in the morning, that his spirit was troubled; and he called for all the seers of Egypt, and all the sages; and Pharaoh told them his dream; but there was no one that could interpret them for Pharaoh.

9. Then the chief butler spoke to Pharaoh, saying: I make mention of my sins today:

10. Pharaoh was angry with his servants, and put me in the custody of the house of the captain of the guard, me and the chief baker.

11. And we dreamed a dream in one night, he and I; we dreamed, each man puzzled over the interpretation of his dream.

12. And there was a young man there with us, a Hebrew, servant to the captain of the guard; and we told him, and he interpreted our dreams; he did interpret for each man according to his dream.

13. And it happened, it was as he interpreted to us: I was restored to mine office, and he was hanged.

14. Then Pharaoh called Joseph, and they brought him quickly out of the dungeon. And he shaved himself, and changed his clothes, and he came in to Pharaoh.

15. And Pharaoh said to Joseph: I have dreamed a dream, and there is no one that can interpret it; and I have heard it said, that when you hear a dream, you can interpret it.

16. And Joseph answered Pharaoh, saying: It is not from me; God will give an answer and peace to Pharaoh.

17. And Pharaoh said to Joseph: In my dream I stood upon the edge of the river.

18. And out of the river came seven cows, healthy fleshed and handsome appearance; and they fed in the reedgrass.

19. And, seven other cows came up after them, poor

and very ill appearance and gaunt fleshed, I have never seen such bad ones in all the land of Egypt.

20. And the gaunt and ill cows ate the first seven fat cows.

21. And when they had eaten them up, you could not tell they had eaten them; but they were still as ill appearing as at the beginning. So, I awoke.

22. And I saw in my dream, seven ears grew on one stalk, full and good.

23. And seven ears, withered, thin, and blasted with the east wind, sprung up after them.

24. And the thin ears swallowed up the seven good ears. And I told it to the seers; but there were none that could tell it to me.

25. And Joseph said to Pharaoh: The dream of Pharaoh is one; God has told to Pharaoh what He is about to do.

26. The seven good cows are seven years; and the seven good ears are seven years: the dream is one.

27. And the seven lean and ill appearing cows that came up after them are seven years, and also the seven empty ears blasted with the east wind; they will be seven years of famine.

28. That is what I said to Pharaoh: God has shown to Pharaoh what He is about to do.

29. So, there will come seven years of great plenty throughout all the land of Egypt.

30. And there will come after them seven years of famine; and all the plenty will be forgotten in the land of Egypt; and the famine will consume the land;

31. And the plenty will not be known in the land because of the famine which follows; because it will be very harsh.

32. And the reason the dream recurred to Pharaoh twice, is because it is established by God, and God will make it happen quickly.

33. Now let Pharaoh find a man discreet and wise, and set him over the land of Egypt.

34. Let Pharaoh do this, and let him appoint overseers over the land, and take one fifth of the [produce of the] land of Egypt in the seven years of plenty.

35. And let them gather all the food of the coming good years, and put the grain under the hand of Pharaoh for food in the cities, and let them keep it.

36. And the food will be a reserve for the land against the seven years of famine, which will be in the land of Egypt; so that the land will not perish through the famine.

37. And this thing was good in the eyes of Pharaoh, and in the eyes of all his servants.

38. And Pharaoh said to his servants: Can we find one like this, a man with the spirit of God?

39. And Pharaoh said to Joseph: Because God has shown you all this, there is no one as discreet and wise as you.

40. You will be over my house, and all my people will be ruled by your word; only in the throne will I be greater than you.

41. And Pharaoh said to Joseph: See, I have set you over all the land of Egypt.

42. And Pharaoh took off his signet ring from his hand, and put it on Joseph's hand, and dressed him in clothes of fine linen, and put a gold chain around his neck.

43. And he had him ride in the second chariot which he had; and they cried before him: **Abrech**; and he set him over all the land of Egypt.

44. And Pharaoh said to Joseph: I am Pharaoh, and without you no man will lift up his hand or his foot in all the land of Egypt.

45. And Pharaoh called Joseph's name Zaphenath-paneah; and he gave him to wife Asenath the daughter of Potiphera priest of On. And Joseph went out over the land of Egypt.

46. And Joseph was thirty years old when he stood before Pharaoh king of Egypt. And Joseph left the presence of Pharaoh, and went throughout all the land of Egypt.

47. And in the seven years of plenty the earth produced in heaps.

48. And he gathered up all the food of the seven years which were in the land of Egypt, and stored the food in the cities; the food of the field, which were around every city, he stored in the same.

49. And Joseph stored grain as the sand of the sea, very much, until they stopped counting; because it was without number.

50. And two sons were born to Joseph before the year of famine came, whom Asenath the daughter of Potiphera priest of on bore to him.

51. And Joseph named the firstborn Manasseh: for God has made me forget all my toil, and all my father's house.

52. And named the second Ephraim: for God has made me fruitful in the land of my affliction.

53. And the seven years of plenty, that were in the land of Egypt, came to an end.

54. And the seven years of famine began, as Joseph had said; and there was famine in all lands; but in all the land of Egypt there was bread.

55. And when all the land of Egypt was famished, the people cried to Pharaoh for bread; and Pharaoh said to all the Egyptians: Go to Joseph; what he says to you, do.

56. And the famine was over all the face of the earth; and Joseph opened all the storehouses, and sold to the Egyptians; and the famine was harsh in the land of Egypt.

57. And all countries came to Egypt to Joseph to buy grain; because the famine was harsh in all the earth.

Chapter 42

1. Now Jacob saw that there was grain in Egypt, and Jacob said to his sons: Why do you stare at each other?

2. And he said: I have heard that there is grain in Egypt. Go down there, and buy for us from there; that we may live, and not die.

3. And Joseph's ten brothers went down to buy grain from Egypt.

4. But Benjamin, Joseph's brother, Jacob did not send with his brothers; for he said: If by chance harm befalls him.

5. And the sons of Israel came to buy among those that came; for the famine was in the land of Canaan.

6. And Joseph was the governor over the land; it was him that sold to all the people of the land. And Joseph's brothers came, and bowed down to him with their faces to the earth.

7. And Joseph saw his brothers, and he knew them, but made himself strange to them, and spoke roughly with them; and he said to them: Why do you come?

And they said: From the land of Canaan to buy food.

8. And Joseph knew his brothers, but they did not know him.

9. And Joseph remembered the dreams which he dreamed of them, and said to them: You are spies; you have come to see the nakedness of the land.

10. And they said to him: No, my lord, your servants have come to buy food.

11. We are all one man's sons; we are upright men; your servants are not spies.

12. And he said to them: No, you have come to see the nakedness of the land.

13. And they said: Your servants are twelve brothers, the sons of one man in the land of Canaan; and, the youngest is with our father today, and one is not.

14. And Joseph said to them: That is it what I said to you, saying: You are spies.

15. So, you will be tested, as Pharaoh lives, you will not leave here, unless your youngest brother comes here.

16. Send one of you, and let him bring your brother, and you will be bound, that your words may be proven, whether there is truth in you; or else, as Pharaoh lives, you are spies.

17. And he put them all together into prison three days.

18. And Joseph said to them on the third day. Do this and live; for I fear God:

19. If you are upright men, let one of your brothers be bound in prison; but go, carry grain for the famine of your houses;

20. And bring your youngest brother to me; so, your words will be verified, and you will not die. And they did.

21. And they said to each other: We are guilty because of our brother, we saw the distress of his soul, when he begged us, and we would not hear; so, this distress has come upon us.

22. And Reuben answered them, saying: Did I not say to you: Do not sin against the boy; and you would not hear? See his blood is required.

23. And they did not know that Joseph understood them; for the interpreter was between them.

24. And he turned himself away from them, and wept; and he returned to them, and spoke to them, and took Simeon from among them, and bound him before their eyes.

25. Then Joseph commanded to fill their vessels with grain, and to restore every man's money into his sack, and to give them provisions for the journey; and it was done to them.

26. And they loaded their donkeys with their grain, and departed from there.

27. And as one of them opened his sack to give his donkey feed in the lodging place, he saw his money; and, it was in the mouth of his sack.

28. And he said to his brothers: My money is restored; and it is in my sack. And their hearts failed them, and they turned trembling each other, saying: What is this that God has done to us?

29. And they came to Jacob their father in the land of Canaan, and told him what had happened to them, saying:

30. The man, the lord of the land, spoke roughly with us, and took us for spies of the country.

31. And we said to him: We are upright men; we are

not spies.

32. We are twelve brothers, sons of our father; one is not, and the youngest is with our father in the land of Canaan.

33. And the man, the lord of the land, said to us: This is how I will know that you are upright men: leave one of your brothers with me, and take grain for the famine of your houses, and go on your way.

34. And bring your youngest brother to me; then I will know that you are no spies, but that you are upright men; so, I will deliver you your brother, and you may travel in the land.

35. And it happened as they emptied their sacks, that, every man's bundle of money was in his sack; and when they and their father saw their bundles of money, they were afraid.

36. And Jacob their father said to them: You have bereaved me: Joseph is no more, and Simeon is no more, and you will take Benjamin away; all these things have come upon me.

37. And Reuben spoke to his father, saying: You may kill my two sons, if I do not bring him to you; deliver him into my hand, and I will bring him back to you.

38. And he said: My son will not go down with you; for his brother is dead, and only he is left; if harm comes to him the way you go, then will you bring down my gray hair with sorrow to the grave.

Chapter 43

1. And the famine was severe in the land.

2. And it happened, when they had eaten the grain which they brought out of Egypt, that their father said to them: Go again, buy us some food.

3. And Judah spoke to him, saying: The man warned us repeatedly, saying: You will not see my face, unless your brother is with you.

4. If you will send our brother with us, we will go down and buy you food;

5. But if you will not send him, we will not go down, because the man said to us: You will not see my face, unless your brother is with you.

6. And Israel said: Why did you deal so poorly with me, to tell the man that you had another brother?

7. And they said: The man asked directly concerning us, and concerning our family, saying: Is your father still alive? Do you have another brother? and we told him according to these words; could we in any way know that he would say: Bring your brother down?

8. And Judah said to Israel his father: Send the boy with me, and we will get up and go, that we may live, and not die, us, and you, and our little ones.

9. I will be a pledge for him; you will require him out of my hand; if I do not bring him to you, and put him in front of you, then let me bear the blame for ever.

10. For if we had not lingered, we had now returned a second time.

11. And their father Israel said to them: If it is so now, do this: take of the choice fruits of the land in your vessels, and carry down the man a present, a little balm, and a little honey, spicery and ladanum, nuts, and almonds;

12. And take double money in your hand; and the money that was returned in the mouth of your sacks carry back in your hand; perhaps it was an oversight;

13. Also, take your brother, and get up, go again to the man;

14. And God Almighty give you mercy before the man, that he may release your other brother and Benjamin to you. And as for me, if I am bereaved of my children, I am bereaved.

15. And the men took that present, and they took double money in their hand, and Benjamin; and got up, and went down to Egypt, and stood before Joseph.

16. And when Joseph saw Benjamin with them, he said to the steward of his house: Bring the men into the house, and kill the animals, and prepare the meat; for the men will dine with me at noon.

17. And the man did as Joseph said; and the man brought the men into Joseph's house.

18. And the men were afraid, because they were brought into Joseph's house; and they said: We are brought in because of the money that was returned in our sacks the first time; that he may seek cause against us, and fall upon us, and take us for slaves, and our donkeys.

19. And they came near to the steward of Joseph's house, and they spoke to him at the door of the house,

20. And said: Oh, my lord, we came down at the first time to buy food.

21. And it happened, when we came to the lodging-place, that we opened our sacks, and, saw every man's money was in the mouth of his sack, our money in full weight; and we have brought it back in our hand.

22. And we have brought other money in our hand to buy food. We do not know who put our money in our sacks.

23. And he said: Peace to you, don't fear; your God, and the God of your father, has given you treasure in your sacks; I had your money. And he brought Simeon out to them.

24. And the man brought the men into Joseph's house, and gave them water, and they washed their feet; and he gave their donkeys feed.

25. And they prepared the present before Joseph's came at noon; for they heard that they would eat bread there.

26. And when Joseph came home, they brought him the present which was in their hand into the house, and bowed down to him to the earth.

27. And he asked them of their welfare, and said: Is your father well, the old man of whom you spoke? Is he still alive?

28. And they said: Your servant our father is well, he is still alive. And they bowed, and declared obeisance.

29. And he lifted up his eyes, and saw Benjamin his brother, his mother's son, and said: Is this your youngest brother of whom you spoke to me? And he said: God be gracious to you, my son.

30. And Joseph made haste; for his heart yearned toward his brother; and he sought a place to weep; and he entered into his chamber, and wept there.

31. And he washed his face, and came out; and he restrained himself, and said: bring the bread.

32. And they set a place for him by himself, and for them by themselves, and for the Egyptians, that ate with him, by themselves; because the Egyptians can not eat bread with the Hebrews; for that is an abomination to the Egyptians.

33. And they sat before him, the firstborn according to his birthright, and the youngest according to his youth; and the men looked at one another surprised.

34. And portions were given to them from before him; but Benjamin's portion was five times as much as any of theirs. And they drank, and were merry with him.

Chapter 44

1. And he commanded the steward of his house, saying: Fill the men's sacks with food, as much as they can carry, and put every man's money in the mouth of his sack.

2. And put my goblet, the silver goblet, in the mouth of the sack of the youngest, and his grain money. And he did what Joseph had spoken.

3. At morning light, the men were sent away, they and their donkeys.

4. And when they were gone from the city, and were not far off, Joseph said to his steward: Get up. Follow after the men; and when you overtake them, say to them: Why have you rewarded good with evil?

5. Is this not what my lord drinks from, and what he divines with? doing this you have done evil.

6. And he overtook them, and he spoke these words to them.

7. And they said to him: Why does my lord speak such words? Impossible! that your servants should do such a thing.

8. Look, the money, which we found in the mouth of our sack, we brought back to you from the land of Canaan; why should we steal silver or gold out of your lord's house?

9. With whoever of your servants it is found, let him die, and we also will be my lord's servants.

10. And he said: Let it be according to your words: he

who has it, will be my bondman; and you will be blameless.

11. Quickly, they put every man's sack to the ground, and opened every man's sack.

12. And he searched, beginning with the eldest, and finishing with the youngest; and the goblet was found in Benjamin's sack.

13. And they tore their clothes, and every man loaded his donkey, and returned to the city.

14. And Judah and his brothers came to Joseph's house, and he was still there; and they fell before him on the ground.

15. And Joseph said to them: What is this thing that you have done? don't you know that a man like me will divine?

16. And Judah said: What can we say to my lord? how can we speak? or how can we clear ourselves? God has found out the crime of your servants; we are my lord's bondmen, we and also in whose hand the cup is found.

17. And he said: I should not do so; the man in whose hand the goblet is found, he will be my servant; but as for you, go in peace to your father.

Vayigash

18. Then Judah came near to him, and said: Oh, my lord, please, let your servant, speak a word in my lord's ears, and do not let your anger burn against your servant; for you are even as Pharaoh.

19. My lord asked his servants, saying: Do you have a father, or a brother?

20. And we said to my lord: We have a father, an old

man, and a child of his old age, a little one; and his brother is dead, and he alone is left of his mother, and his father loves him.

21. And you said to your servants: Bring him down to me, that I may set my eyes upon him.

22. And we said to my lord: The boy cannot leave his father; for if he should leave his father, his father would die.

23. And you said to your servants: Unless your youngest brother comes down with you, you will see my face no more.

24. And it happened when we came up to your servant my father, we told him the words of my lord.

25. And our father said: Go again, buy us some food.

26. And we said: We cannot go down; if our youngest brother is with us, then will we go down; for we may not see the man's face, unless our youngest brother is with us.

27. And your servant my father said to us: You know that my wife bore me two sons;

28. And the one left me, and I said: Surely, he is torn in pieces; and I have not seen him since;

29. And if you also take this one from me, and harm befalls him, you will bring down my gray head with sorrow to the grave.

30. Now when I come to your servant my father, and the boy is not with us; seeing that his soul is bound up with the boy's soul;

31. It will happen, when he sees that the boy is not with us, that he will die; and your servants will bring down the gray head of your servant our father with sorrow to the grave.

32. For your servant became a guarantee for the boy

to my father, saying: If I do not bring him to you, then I will bear the blame to my father for ever.

33. Now, please, let your servant, stay instead of the boy a servant to my lord; and let the boy go up with his brothers.

34. For how will I go up to my father, if the boy is not with me? in case I look upon the evil that will come on my father.

Chapter 45

1. Then Joseph could not restrain himself before all that stood near him; and he cried: Make every man go away from me. And no man stood there with him, while Joseph made himself known to his brothers.

2. And he wept out loud; and the Egyptians heard, and the house of Pharaoh heard.

3. And Joseph said to his brothers: I am Joseph; does my father still live? And his brothers could not answer him; because they were frighted at his presence.

4. And Joseph said to his brother: Please, come near to me. And they came near. And he said: I am Joseph your brother, who you sold into Egypt.

5. And now do not grieve, or be angry with yourselves, that you sold me here; for God sent me before you to preserve life.

6. For two years famine has been in the land; and there are still five years, in which there will be no plowing or harvest.

7. And God sent me before you to give you a remnant on the earth, and to save you alive for a great deliverance.

8. So now it was not you that sent me here, but God;

and He has made me a father to Pharaoh, and lord of all his house, and ruler over all the land of Egypt.

9. Quickly, go up to my father, and say to him: Your son Joseph says: God has made me lord of all Egypt; come down to me, do not delay.

10. And you will dwell in the land of Goshen, and you will be near me, you, and your children, and your children's children, and your flocks, and your herds, and all that you have;

11. And there will I sustain you; for there are still five years of famine; to prevent you coming to poverty, you, and your household, and all that you have.

12. And, your eyes see, and the eyes of my brother Benjamin, that it is my mouth that speaks to you.

13. And you will tell my father of all my glory in Egypt, and of all that you have seen; and you will quickly bring down my father here.

14. And he fell upon his brother Benjamin's neck, and wept; and Benjamin wept upon his neck.

15. And he kissed all his brothers, and wept upon them; and after that his brothers talked with him.

16. And the report was heard in Pharaoh's house, saying: Joseph's brothers have come; and it pleased Pharaoh, and his servants.

17. And Pharaoh said to Joseph: Say to your brothers: Do this: load your beasts, and go to the land of Canaan;

18. And take your father and your households, and come to me; and I will give you the best land of Egypt, and you will eat the fat of the land.

19. Now you are commanded, do this: take wagons out of the land of Egypt for your little ones, and for your wives, and bring your father, and come.

20. Also don't worry about your things; for the good things of all the land of Egypt are yours.

21. And the sons of Israel did; and Joseph gave them wagons, according to the command of Pharaoh, and gave them provisions for the way.

22. To all of them he gave each man changes of clothes; but he gave three hundred shekels of silver to Benjamin, and five changes of clothes.

23. And to his father he sent ten donkeys loaded with the good things of Egypt, and ten she-donkeys loaded with grain and bread and food for his father for the way.

24. So, he sent his brothers away, and they departed; and he said to them: See that you do not get angry on the way.

25. And they went up out of Egypt, and came into the land of Canaan to Jacob their father.

26. And they told him, saying: Joseph is still alive, and he is ruler over all the land of Egypt. And his heart became numb, for he did not believe them.

27. And they told him all the words of Joseph, which he had said to them; and when he saw the wagons which Joseph had sent to carry him, the spirit of Jacob their father revived.

28. And Israel said: It is enough; Joseph my son is still alive; I will go and see him before I die.

Chapter 46

1. And Israel with all that he had, went on his journey and came to Beersheba, and offered sacrifices to the God of his father Isaac.

2. And God spoke to Israel in the visions of the night, and said: Jacob, Jacob. And he said: Here am I.

3. And He said: I am God, the God of your father; do not fear to go down to Egypt; for there, I will make you a great nation.

4. I will go down with you into Egypt; and I will also certainly bring you up again; and Joseph will put his hand upon your eyes.

5. And Jacob rose up from Beer-sheba; and the sons of Israel carried Jacob their father, and their little ones, and their wives, in the wagons which Pharaoh had sent to carry him.

6. And they took their cattle, and their goods, which they had obtained in the land of Canaan, and came to Egypt, Jacob, and all his seed with him;

7. His sons, and his sons' sons with him, his daughters, and his sons' daughters, and all his seed brought he with him into Egypt.

8. And these are the names of the children of Israel, who came to Egypt, Jacob and his sons: Reuben, Jacob's first-born.

9. And the sons of Reuben: Hanoch, and Pallu, and Hezron, and Carmi.

10. And the sons of Simeon: Jemuel, and Jamin, and Ohad, and Jachin, and Zohar, and Shaul the son of a Canaanitish woman.

11. And the sons of Levi: Gershon, Kohath, and Merari.

12. And the sons of Judah: Er, and Onan, and Shelah, and Perez, and Zerah; but Er and Onan died in the land of Canaan. And the sons of Perez were Hezron and Hamul.

13. And the sons of Issachar: Tola, and Puvah, and Iob, and Shimron.

14. And the sons of Zebulun: Sered, and Elon, and

Jahleel.

15. These are the sons of Leah, who she bore to Jacob in Paddan-aram, with his daughter Dinah; all the souls of his sons and his daughters were thirty-three.

16. And the sons of Gad: Ziphion, and Haggi, Shuni, and Ezbon, Eri, and Arodi, and Areli.

17. And the sons of Asher: Imnah, and Ishvah, and Ishvi, and Beriah, and Serah their sister; and the sons of Beriah: Heber, and Malchiel.

18. These are the sons of Zilpah, who Laban gave to Leah his daughter, and these she bore to Jacob, sixteen souls.

19. The sons of Rachel Jacob's wife: Joseph and Benjamin.

20. And to Joseph in the land of Egypt were born Manasseh and Ephraim, who Asenath the daughter of Potiphera priest of on bore to him.

21. And the sons of Benjamin: Bela, and Becher, and Ashbel, Gera, and Naaman, Ehi, and Rosh, Muppim, and Huppim, and Ard.

22. These are the sons of Rachel, who were born to Jacob; all the souls were fourteen.

23. And the sons of Dan: Hushim.

24. And the sons of Naphtali: Jahzeel, and Guni, and Jezer, and Shillem.

25. These are the sons of Bilhah, who Laban gave to Rachel his daughter, and these she bore to Jacob; all the souls were seven.

26. All the souls belonging to Jacob that came into Egypt, that came out of him, besides Jacob's sons' wives, all the souls were sixty-six.

27. And the sons of Joseph, who were born to him in Egypt, were two souls; all the souls of the house of

Jacob, that came into Egypt, were seventy.

28. And he sent Judah before him to Joseph, to show the him way to Goshen; and they came to the land of Goshen.

29. And Joseph prepared his chariot, and went up to meet Israel his father, in Goshen; and he presented himself to him, and fell on his neck, and wept on his neck a good while.

30. And Israel said to Joseph: Now let me die, since I have seen your face, that you are still alive.

31. And Joseph said to his brothers, and to his father's house: I will go up, and tell Pharaoh, and will say to him: My brothers, and my father's house, who were in the land of Canaan, have come to me;

32. And the men are shepherds, for they have been keepers of cattle; and they have brought their flocks, and their herds, and all that they have.

33. And it will happen, when Pharaoh will call you, and will say: What is your occupation?

34. That you will say: Your servants have been keepers of cattle from our youth even until now, both we, and our fathers; that you may dwell in the land of Goshen; for every shepherd is an abomination to the Egyptians.

Chapter 47

1. Then Joseph went and told Pharaoh, and said: My father and my brothers, and their flocks, and their herds, and all that they own, have come out of the land of Canaan; and, they are in the land of Goshen.

2. And he took five men from among his brothers, and presented them to Pharaoh.

3. And Pharaoh said to his brothers: What is your

occupation? And they said to Pharaoh: Your servants are shepherds, both we, and our fathers.

4. And they said to Pharaoh: we have come to sojourn in the land; for there is no pasture for your servants' flocks; for the famine is severe in the land of Canaan. Now please, let your servants live in the land of Goshen.

5. And Pharaoh spoke to Joseph, saying: Your father and your brothers have come to you;

6. The land of Egypt is before you; in the best of the land make you father and your brothers to dwell; in the land of Goshen let them live. And if you know any able men among them, then make them shepherds over my cattle.

7. And Joseph brought in Jacob his father, and put him before Pharaoh. And Jacob blessed Pharaoh.

8. And Pharaoh said to Jacob: How many are the days of the years of your life?

9. And Jacob said to Pharaoh: The days of the years of my sojourning's are a hundred thirty years; few and evil have been the days of the years of my life, and they have not matched the days of the years of the lives of my fathers in the days of their sojourning's.

10. And Jacob blessed Pharaoh, and went out from the presence of Pharaoh.

11. And Joseph placed his father and his brethren, and gave them a possession in the land of Egypt, in the best of the land, in the land of Rameses, as Pharaoh had commanded.

12. And Joseph sustained his father, and his brothers, and all his father's household, with bread, satisfying the hunger of their little ones.

13. And there was no bread in all the land; for the

famine was very severe, so that the land of Egypt and the land of Canaan suffered because of the famine.

14. And Joseph gathered up all the money that was found in the land of Egypt, and in the land of Canaan, for the grain which they bought; and Joseph brought the money into Pharaoh's house.

15. And when the money was all spent in the land of Egypt, and in the land of Canaan, all the Egyptians came to Joseph, and said: Give us bread; for why should we die in your presence because our money is spent.

16. And Joseph said: Give your cattle, and I will give you [bread] for your cattle, if money is spent.

17. And they brought their cattle to Joseph. And Joseph gave them bread in exchange for the horses, and for the flocks, and for the herds, and for the asses; and he fed them with bread in exchange for all their cattle for that year.

18. And when that year ended, they came to him the second year, and said to him: We will not hide from my lord, how that our money is all spent; and the herds of cattle are my lord's; there is nothing left in the sight of my lord, but our bodies, and our lands.

19. Why should we die before thine eyes, we and our land? buy us and our land for bread, and we and our land will be servants to Pharaoh; and give us seed, so we may live, and not die, and that the land not be desolate.

20. So, Joseph bought all the land of Egypt for Pharaoh; because every Egyptians sold his field, because the famine was severe on them; and the land became Pharaoh's.

21. And as for the people, he removed them city by

city, from one end of the border of Egypt even to the other end of it.

22. He did not buy the land of the priests alone, because the priests had a portion from Pharaoh, and ate their portion which Pharaoh gave them; This is why they did not sell their land.

23. Then Joseph said to the people: I have bought you today and your land for Pharaoh. Here are seed for you, and you will sow the land.

24. And it will happen at the harvest, that you will give a fifth to Pharaoh, and four parts will be your own, for seed of the field, and for your food, and for your households, and for food for your little ones.

25. And they said: You have saved our lives. Let us find favor in the sight of my lord, and we will be Pharaoh's servants.

26. And Joseph made it a statute concerning the land of Egypt to this day, that Pharaoh should have the fifth; only the land of the priests was not Pharaoh's.

27. And Israel lived in the land of Egypt, in the land of Goshen; and they obtained possessions in it, and were fruitful, and multiplied greatly.

Vayechi

28. And Jacob lived in the land of Egypt seventeen years; so, the days of Jacob, the years of his life, were a hundred forty-seven years.

29. And the time drew near that Israel must die; and he called his son Joseph, and said to him: If now I have found favor in your sight, please put your hand under my thigh, and deal kindly and truly with me; please do not bury me in Egypt.

30. But when I sleep with my fathers, you will carry me out of Egypt, and bury me in their burial place. And he said: I will do as you have said.

31. And he said: **Swear to me**. And he swore to him. And Israel bowed down upon the bed's head.

Chapter 48

1. And it happened after these things, that one said to Joseph: **Your father is sick**. And he took with him his two sons, Manasseh and Ephraim.

2. And one told Jacob, and said: Your son Joseph comes to you. And Israel strengthened himself, and sat upon the bed.

3. And Jacob said to Joseph: God Almighty appeared unto me at Luz in the land of Canaan, and blessed me,

4. And said to me: I will make you fruitful, and multiply you, and I will make of you a company of peoples; and will give this land to your seed after you for an everlasting possession.

5. And now your two sons, who were born to you in the land of Egypt before I came to you in Egypt, are mine; Ephraim and Manasseh, even as Reuben and Simeon, will be mine.

6. And your issue, that you produce after them, will be yours; they will be called by the name of their brothers in their inheritance.

7. And as for me, when I came from Paddan, Rachel died from me in the land of Canaan in the way, when there was still some way to come unto Ephrath; and I buried her there on the way to Ephrath - also called Bethlehem.

8. And Israel saw Joseph's sons, and said: Who are these?

9. And Joseph said to his father: They are my sons, who God has given me here. And he said: Bring them to me, please, and I will bless them.

10. Now the eyes of Israel were dim with age, so that he could not see. And he brought them near to him; and he kissed them, and embraced them.

11. And Israel said to Joseph: I had not thought I would see your face; and, God has let me see your seed also.

12. And Joseph brought them out from between his knees; and he fell down on his face to the earth.

13. And Joseph took them both, Ephraim in his right hand toward Israel's left hand, and Manasseh in his left hand toward Israel's right hand, and brought them near to him.

14. And Israel stretched out his right hand, and laid it on Ephraim's head, who was the younger, and his left hand on Manasseh's head, guiding his hands intentionally; for Manasseh was the first-born.

15. And he blessed Joseph, and said: The God my fathers Abraham and Isaac walked before, the God who has been my shepherd all my life to this day,

16. The angel who has redeemed me from all evil, bless the boys; and let my name be named in them, and the name of my fathers Abraham and Isaac; and let them grow into a multitude in the midst of the earth.

17. And when Joseph saw that his father was laying his right hand on the head of Ephraim, it displeased him, and he held up his father's hand, to remove it from Ephraim's head to Manasseh's head.

18. And Joseph said to his father: Not so, my father, for this is the firstborn; put your right hand on his head.

19. And his father refused, and said: I know it, my son, I know it; he will also become a people, and he will also be great; but his younger brother will be greater than him, and his seed shall become a multitude of nations.

20. And he blessed them that day, saying: By you Israel will bless, saying: God make you as Ephraim and as Manasseh. And he set Ephraim before Manasseh.

21. And Israel said to Joseph: I die; but God will be with you, and bring you back to the land of your fathers.

22. Also, I have given you one portion above your brothers, which I took out of the hand of the Amorite with my sword and with my bow.

Chapter 49

1. And Jacob called to his sons, and said: Gather yourselves together, that I may tell you that which will happen to you in the end of days.

2. Assemble yourselves, and hear me, sons of Jacob; And listen to Israel your father.

3. Reuben, you are my first-born, My might, and the first-fruits of my strength; Above the others in dignity, and above [the others] in power.

4. Unstable as water, you will not be above the others; Because you went to your father's bed; Then you defiled it - he went up to my couch.

5. Simeon and Levi are brothers; Weapons of violence their kinship.

6. Do not let my soul come into their council; Do not let my glory be united to their assembly; For in their anger, they killed men, and in their selfishness, they maimed oxen.

7. Cursed is their anger, because it was fierce, and their wrath, because it was cruel; I will divide them in Jacob, and scatter them in Israel

8. Judah, your brothers will praise you; Your hand will be on the neck of your enemies; Your father's sons will bow down before you.

9. Judah is a lion's cub; From the prey, my son, you left. He stooped down, he crouched like a lion, and like a lioness; who will wake him?

10. The sceptre will not depart from Judah, Nor the ruler's staff from between his feet. As long as men come to Shiloh; And to him the obedience of the peoples.

11. Binding his foal to the vine, and his donkey's colt to the choice vine; He washes his clothes in wine, And his covering in the blood of grapes;

12. His eyes will be red with wine, And his teeth white with milk.

13. Zebulun will live at the shore of the sea, and he will be a port for ships, and his flank will be on Zidon.

14. Issachar is a large-boned ass, Crouching down between the two folds.

15. For he saw a resting place that was good, And the land that was pleasant; And he bowed his shoulder to bear, and became a servant under task

16. Dan will judge his people. As one of the tribes of Israel.

17. Dan will be a serpent in the road, A horned snake in the path, that bites the horse's heels, so that his rider falls backward.

18. I wait for Your salvation, O Lord.

19. Gad, an army will march upon him; But he will march upon their heel.

20. As for Asher, his bread will be fat, and he will yield royal foods.

21. Naphtali is a hind let loose: He gives good words.

22. Joseph is a fruitful vine, A fruitful vine by a fountain; Its branches run over the wall.

23. The archers have dealt bitterly with him, and shot at him, and hated him;

24. But his bow held firm, And the arms of his hands were made strong, By the hands of the Mighty One of Jacob, From there, from the Shepherd, the Stone of Israel,

25. Even by the God of your father, who will help you, and by the Almighty, who will bless you. With blessings of heaven above, Blessings of the deep that lay beneath, Blessings of the breasts, and of the womb.

26. The blessings of your father Are mighty beyond the blessings of my progenitors to the end boundaries of the everlasting hills; They will be on the head of Joseph, And on the crown of the head of the prince among his brothers.

27. Benjamin is a ravenous wolf; In the morning he devours the prey, and in the evening, he divides the spoil.

28. All these are the twelve tribes of Israel, and this is it how their father spoke to them and blessed them; he blessed them each according to his blessing.

29. And he charged them, and said to them: I am to be gathered to my people; bury me with my fathers in the cave that is in the field of Ephron the Hittite,

30. In the cave that is in the field of Machpelah, which is before Mamre, in the land of Canaan, which Abraham bought with the field from Ephron the Hittite for a burial place.

31. There they buried Abraham and Sarah his wife; there they buried Isaac and Rebekah his wife; and there I buried Leah.

32. The field and the cave that is in it, which was purchased from the children of Heth.

33. And when Jacob finished commanding his sons, he pulled his feet into the bed, and died, and was gathered to his people.

Chapter 50

1. And Joseph fell on his father's face, and wept on him, and kissed him.

2. And Joseph commanded his servants the physicians to embalm his father. And the physicians embalmed Israel.

3. And forty days were fulfilled for him; for so are fulfilled the days of embalming. And the Egyptians wept for him seventy days.

4. And when the days of weeping for him were past, Joseph spoke to the house of Pharaoh, saying: If I have found favor in your eyes, please speak, to Pharaoh, saying:

5. My father made me swear, saying: I die; in my grave which I have prepared in the land of Canaan, you will bury me there. Now please, let me go up, and bury my father, and I will come back.

6. And Pharaoh said: Go up, and bury your father, as he made you swear.

7. And Joseph went up to bury his father; and all the servants of Pharaoh went up with him, the elders of his house, and all the elders of the land of Egypt,

8. And all the house of Joseph, and his brothers, and his father's house; the left only their little ones, and their flocks, and their herds, in the land of Goshen.

9. And chariots and horsemen went up with him; and it was a very large assembly.

10. And they came to the threshing-floor of Atad, which is beyond the Jordan, and there they wailed with a very great and sore wailing; and he mourned for his father seven days.

11. And when the inhabitants of the land, the Canaanites, saw the mourning in the floor of Atad, they said: This is a grievous mourning to the Egyptians. So, it was named Abel-mizraim, which is beyond the Jordan.

12. And his sons did as he commanded them.

13. For his sons carried him into the land of Canaan, and buried him in the cave of the field of Machpelah, which Abraham bought with the field, for a burial place, from Ephron the Hittite, in front of Mamre.

14. And Joseph returned to Egypt, he, and his brothers, and all who went up with him to bury his father, after he had buried his father.

15. And when Joseph's brothers saw that their father was dead, they said: Maybe Joseph will hate us, and will pay back all the evil which we did to him.

16. And they sent a message to Joseph, saying: Your father commanded before he died, saying:

17. You will say to Joseph: Please, forgive the transgression of your brothers, and their sin, for the evil that they did to you. And now, please forgive the transgression of the servants of the God of your father. And Joseph wept when they spoke to him.

18. And his brothers also went and fell down before his face; and they said: **We are your servants**.

19. And Joseph said to them: Do not fear; am I in the place of God?

20. And as for you, you meant evil against me; but God meant it for good, to bring about what has happened today, to keep many people alive.

21. So, do not fear; I will sustain you, and your little ones. And he comforted them, and spoke kindly to them.

22. And Joseph lived in Egypt, he, and his father's house; and Joseph lived a hundred and ten years.

23. And Joseph saw Ephraim's children of the third generation; the children also of Machir the son of Manasseh were born upon Joseph's knees.

24. And Joseph said to his brothers: I die; but God will remember you, and bring you up out of this land to the land which He swore to Abraham, to Isaac, and to Jacob.

25. And Joseph took an oath of the children of Israel, saying: God will surely remember you, and you will carry up my bones from here.

26. So, Joseph died, being a hundred ten years old. And they embalmed him, and he was put in a coffin in Egypt.